*Beyond Healing*

# Beyond Healing

*Jennifer Rees Larcombe*

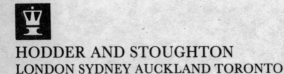

**HODDER AND STOUGHTON**
LONDON SYDNEY AUCKLAND TORONTO

Bible quotations are taken from the Good News Bible unless otherwise stated.

**British Library Cataloguing in Publication Data**

Larcombe, Jennifer Rees
   Beyond healing.—(Hodder Christian paperbacks)
   1. Christian Life
   I. Title
   248.4      BV4501.2

ISBN 0 340 39126 X

*Published by Hodder and Stoughton, a division of Hodder and Stoughton Ltd, Mill Road, Dunton Green, Sevenoaks, Kent TN13 2YA. Editorial Office: 47 Bedford Square, London WC1B 3DP*

*Photoset by Hewer Text Composition Services, Edinburgh.*
*Printed in Great Britain by Cox and Wyman Ltd, Reading.*

## Foreword

Faith, pushed beyond limits, may be forced to cry, 'Why?'

Still, if God chooses to remain silent, faith is content.

Why was so choice a servant of God as Amy Carmichael of India required to spend the last twenty years of her life in bed and frequently in pain as the result of an accident? It was during those years that she wrote books that have become priceless classics to those who know and love them.

Why did George Matheson have to lose his eyesight? Yet what would we do without the hymn born out of his suffering, 'Oh Love that wilt not let me go . . .'

One could well question the incomprehensible sufferings of Job. Yet how many down through the centuries have had their own faith strengthened in the face of insurmountable trials, by Job's unquenchable faith?

Suffering can be a hideous thing, frustrating, debilitating and apparently wasteful of useful, fulfilling lives.

And yet God, in His sovereignty, still permits illness.

The pressure to seek healing can lay heavy burdens of guilt on the ones God does not choose to heal.

Like the Psalmist in Psalm 55:6, many of us are pressured to pray, 'O that I had wings of a dove then would I fly away . . .' (or 'Let me out of here!') while others wait patiently on the Lord and find their strength renewed as He promised in Isaiah 40:31. So there is the choice: 'away' or 'up'.

Here is a book for us all, written by one who knows whereof she speaks. Jen has been a dear friend for years, as her parents were before her. If anyone deserved to be healed it was Jen. But it could be that Jen, like God's medal of honour heroes in the last of Hebrews 11, will not receive the promise of deliverance, 'God having some better thing for us.'

I look for the book to be a part of that 'better thing'.

Ruth Bell Graham

## Preface

This book is about a family, not just me. We have talked and prayed together over it, knowing that it will mean the end of some of our privacy and all of our pride. None of us comes out of it very well. But because we know now that Christians are not superstars, we want to give an honest account of how God carried an ordinary husband and wife and their six children through three traumatic years. If any of the eight of us had not wanted to be that open to the public, this book could never have been written.

Many other people have allowed themselves to be mentioned. They would much rather not have been, but they wanted to show how God works. People like John the tramp, our pastor Brian Hill, Eunja who dreamed I was going to die, and was brave enough to tell me so, and Grace who did so much without being asked and who taught me how to pray.

When our marriage threatened to disintegrate under the strain, it was our friends Hugh and Ginny O'Connor who introduced us to Dave and Joyce Ames and between them they helped us to put our relationship back together again.

The miracle of the love and care I was given at Burrswood, paid for by so many godly Christians, remains a precious memory. God even sent us a Christian consultant and doctor, and we know that we are regularly prayed for by them both. God can really work through them unhindered.

This book couldn't have been written without the gift from an anonymous friend who gave me an especially adapted typewriter which I can use lying down. It was a jumbled mass at first, but then my cousin Tanya Aydon promised me she'd tidy it up. So with her experience on *Today* magazine, together with our shared love of God and similar sense of humour we decided to work at it together. Her mother, my greatly loved Auntie Gerry, took charge of her baby son Tom, while we hacked the tangle of weeds into shape. I could never have done this book without them both.

As a final guard, the Rev. George Swannell, who as Chaplain of the Kent and Sussex Hospital supported me throughout the worst patches of my illness, checked for any dreadful theological errors that might have crept in.

I want to thank all these people – and also countless others whose sacrificial love and prayer have constantly surrounded us and lifted us up towards God.

# Chapter One

The telephone rang as it always does at the most inconvenient moment possible – just when lunch was ready. My husband Tony was at the furthest end of the garden where men go when you want them to carve a joint, so I gave the saucepans an irritated shove to the back of the stove and picked up the receiver. It was Eunja, a Korean Christian friend of ours, and she sounded upset.

'Jen, I just don't know whether I should have rung you or not,' she began, 'but Charles and I have prayed so much this morning and we feel that I should tell you something.' She sounded as if she was crying, but my mind was still with the Yorkshire puddings – my watch told me that in just four minutes they would start to burn.

'What's up?' I asked, trying not to sound hassled.

'Well,' she began, 'God often shows me things in dreams. Last night, I had a terrible dream about you. I dreamt you were going to die soon.'

I felt as if someone had kicked me very hard in the tummy and I sat down heavily on the bottom of the stairs.

'It probably doesn't mean anything,' she added quickly, 'but do pray about it, won't you.'

That was doubtless very good advice, but I did no such thing. As I put the phone down I felt very angry. 'God doesn't frighten people with forecasts of doom,' I raged to myself, as I watched the custard boil all over the stove. 'All this is a load of spoofy codswallop!'

'God used dreams a lot in the Bible,' said a small voice

inside my head, but I refused to listen, and was very bad-tempered with the children for the rest of the day.

All the same, I was badly frightened by that telephone call. It had come much too soon after a horrible nightmare of my own. Just a few nights before I had dreamed that something terrible was going to happen to our family, but I had woken in a cold sweat of terror before finding out what it was. I'd been so frightened I'd had to creep down to the kitchen and put the kettle on. As I had sipped my tea a wave of relief swept over me. It had only been a silly dream after all. Nothing was going to spoil the life I enjoyed so much.

I had every reason to be happy and I was. We lived in an idyllic Sussex village where I knew everyone. They all knew me as 'that mad fat woman with herds of kids', for not only did I have my own large family but I was a foster mother and also 'minded' several other children on a daily basis. Our home was down a little lane, surrounded by woods and fields. We kept hens, grew our own vegetables and made our own bread. I cooked cakes for every village function and dashed happily round the district doing things for people whether they really wanted me to or not.

Looking back I am horrified at how irritating I must have been! There can be something vaguely unsympathetic about Christian families apparently living in permanent sunshine, and we certainly appeared to have everything. Our marriage and home were secure, our children were healthy, Tony's job as a teacher adviser was reasonably paid and we were involved and appreciated at our little local church. It was the sort of lifestyle that others might envy, but I was so happy and busy that the idea never occurred to me.

I never even thought of the dream when I woke next morning with the feeling that something nice was going to happen. I'd had the morning marked in my diary with a large red cross for days. I was going to Firtoll Woods, and I had a very special appointment there. In a few months I was going to be forty, and by then Richard, our youngest son, would be at

10

school all day. I had the delicious assurance that something exciting was going to happen.

After fourteen solid years of motherhood I felt I was about to reach a new beginning and was convinced that child-rearing was only a prelude to the real business of life. What did God want to do with my time: surely not spend it just cleaning loos and peeling potatoes and looking after other people's children?

I was beginning to get a number of invitations to speak at coffee mornings and lunches run by Christian women who wanted their friends and neighbours to hear about what God has done for us. It would be fun driving off in the car and meeting lots of new interesting people after years of baby talk, but was it right to do that and be a mother?

Before I said 'yes' to any more of these invitations, I really wanted to talk the whole thing over with God and ask Him to tell me what to do, but I had to go out if I wanted to do that. I knew only too well that if I knelt down to pray at home, I would think: I could be doing the ironing, or Why don't I knock up the dough before Richard comes back from play-group and 'helps' me. The phone would ring or a friend would pop round for a coffee. No, if I wanted to be quite alone with God, I had to go out.

A few minutes after waving goodbye to Richard at the playgroup door, I was happily pulling on my wellingtons and gloating over the memory of the wonderful times I had enjoyed with God in this lovely wood. I remembered the pungent scent of the bluebells, the way the sunlight flickered through the beech leaves and dappled the water in the little stream. It had been so easy to communicate with God amongst such beauty.

But I was in for a nasty shock that morning. Of course, I really couldn't expect bluebells in late February, and the once lovely leaves lay rotting and mouldy on the ground, smelling of death and decay. It was a dark, dismal morning and the rain splashed down on my soggy hat through the bare branches. I splashed miserably along by the muddy stream dictating what sounded like a shopping list of requests to God who felt too far away to hear anyway.

At last I sat down on a crumbling tree stump and gave up even trying to pray. But then God spoke to me instead. I didn't hear a voice or see a vision, but I knew He was speaking all right. The first time that had ever happened to me I had been skinning a tomato and I was so surprised I dropped it – splat – on to the kitchen floor! When God is really speaking to me, there is no doubt whatever in my mind that it is His voice I can hear. If ever I think, That's just my imagination, and I do not have that clear certainty, I know it *is* only me talking and not God at all.

This time it was unmistakable.

'Your life has been like this wood was in the springtime,' He said. 'If it became bleak, lifeless and wintry could you still praise Me?'

'I don't know, Lord,' I replied out loud, feeling rather startled.

'In Heaven,' He continued, 'your life will always be like the woods in May time.'

That was *not* the kind of thing I wanted to hear. I had expected some great commissioning from Him. Whenever I scrubbed the kitchen floor I imagined myself as a female evangelist popping on and off jet planes to address vast conventions of women all over the world. After all, both my parents had been evangelists, and I felt sure I would be called to be one as well.

But as I sat hunched on my damp tree stump I suddenly remembered my dream of the night before, and felt very cold. The memory of the 'terrible thing' that was going to engulf us made me shiver and I went home rather hastily to put the kettle on, and write down exactly what God had said in the little black diary I have been keeping for the last few years.

'I don't understand you, Lord,' I muttered as I hurtled into the car to meet Richard, but as I shot down the lane I found myself singing a chorus we have sometimes at church. It's just a few verses from Habakkuk set to a bouncy tune:

> Although the fig tree does not blossom
> and there be no fruit on the vine,
> The produce of the olive fail,
> and the fields yield no corn,
> The flock shall be cut off from the fold,
> and there be no herd in the stall,
> Yet will I rejoice in the Lord,
> and I will joy in the God of my salvation.
> (Based on Hab. 3: 17–18)

As usual, I was disgraced by being 'last Mummy' at the playgroup, but yet again Richard's huge bear hug showed me he had forgiven me and I was soon caught up in the whirl of the rest of the week and forgot my dreams and fancies – until Saturday morning and Eunja's telephone call.

Fear becomes bigger and bigger when it is not faced and as I tried to run away from mine, I was forgetting that when God provided us with armour to protect us from attacks by the enemy (Eph. 6: 10–13) He gave us none for our backs, so we deserve all we get when we panic and run.

The next few days as I spring-cleaned the house and did loads of unnecessary washing, I knew full well I was just being busy on purpose. When Tuesday evening came and I realised I would be alone because Tony was away at a conference for maths teachers, I surrounded myself with a huge pile of long-overdue mending, and turned on the television very loudly. But it was no good. My stomach was churning, I had reached the end of the road.

'I must talk this over with someone,' I said, as I hurled a half-darned sock across the room, 'but who can I ring up this late in the evening?'

How can it be that a person who has known and loved the Lord for as many years as I have, when faced with a problem always thinks, Whose advice can I ask? or What book could

I read for help? When will I learn to go straight to God Himself, for whenever I do that He either removes the problem, changes my reaction to it, or sends along just the right person to help. Fortunately, it *was* far too late to ring anyone that evening, so I got down on my knees among the mending and said, 'Lord, I must talk to you, I'm terribly frightened'.

'Are you *really* frightened of dying?' was His instant reply. I thought that through carefully and then replied, 'No Lord, I definitely am *not* frightened of being dead because I know I'll come straight to Heaven and meet you there.'

There was no doubt whatever in my mind about that. It might sound rather presumptuous, and I once deeply shocked a neighbour of mine by saying that to her as we stood in the queue for fish at Heathfield market.

'How can you possibly be sure you're good enough to go to Heaven?' she had demanded.

'Well I know for certain I'm *not* good enough and never will be,' I replied over the fillets of plaice, 'and all the wrong things I do *should* separate me from God completely. That's why Jesus came to earth and died on the cross to be blamed and punished for my sins, and because I've accepted what He did for me I know for sure I'll make Heaven.' She looked so shocked that I could not help adding, 'If Heaven was going to be full of "goodie goodies" who felt they had a right to be there because of their good behaviour it would be so boring I'd rather go to the other place!' Quite horrified, she ordered sole instead of her usual coley – we have often laughed about it since.

But I wasn't laughing that Tuesday evening. No, I was not frightened of *being* dead, but the actual dying bit bothered me. What would it feel like? And then I remembered Tony and the children. Like all mums I thought I was quite indispensable. It was our foster daughter Janie who worried me far more than the other five. Both her mother and father were dead, and we had looked after her as part of our family since she was seven. Watching both her parents die had given her a terror of illness, and I only had to sneeze for her to

14

panic. Once when the central heating broke down and I crossly said I was sure I'd die of the cold, her two little hands clutched my woolly jumper like clammy starfish for the rest of the day. Her little life had been so shattered that it had taken nearly five years to piece her together with prayer. Surely, I thought as I knelt among the mending, God couldn't allow a third tragedy to envelope her.

'You can trust me for yourself,' the Lord seemed to say, 'why can't you trust me for the children?' It is strange, but that always does seem harder to do.

I picked up Tony's half-darned sock and hoped he'd marry again quickly. I knew just the right person, and had a sneaking suspicion that she'd make him a far better wife anyway. Should I write him a note to point out her obvious virtues? That started me giggling – what if I didn't die after all and he found the note one day, what a fool I'd look. I laughed so much I felt loads better, and when I had committed the whole thing to the Lord, I went off to bed in peace.

A very wonderful thing happened to me two days later at our House Group meeting. Although we met at the home of our pastor, Brian Hill, the group was open to anyone, and not confined to our church members. So there was Dr Jordan from the parish church, Mr and Mrs Burton who were very elderly Strict Baptists, and Brother Tom – a Roman Catholic monk and the cook in a small community in our village. Once a bad-tempered old man with a habit of swearing loudly and frequently, he was now one of the most joy-filled people I have ever met, and all because of a remarkable encounter with God in his cell one night.

Those Thursday evenings were the high spot of the week as about a dozen of us met to read the Bible and pray. Because we all came from such different backgrounds, we enjoyed discovering the many important areas where we agreed. Mrs Burton's incredible knowledge of the Bible, gained by eighty years of close study, amazed Brother Tom – while she was equally intrigued by his accounts of what the Lord said to him while he cooked in the monastery kitchen.

15

'Surely, God only speaks to us through His scriptures,' Mrs Burton said one night. 'You talk as if He chatted to you all day long,' she added rather wistfully.

'So He does, dear Mrs Burton,' replied the old monk, his eyes twinkling. 'He would never contradict His holy scriptures, but why should He not speak to me direct, as I can speak to Him?' The two of them had many heated arguments about speaking in tongues and the Virgin Mary, but they both loved the Lord they recognised in one another.

During a quiet period of prayer that particular Thursday evening, I was startled to hear Brother Tom speaking my name. I had told no one except the Lord and my black diary about the fears I had faced that week, but suddenly Brother Tom said, 'Jen, the Lord tells me to say that you are released from your fear!'

I was overcome with relief and joy. So I wasn't going to die after all. It had just been a test to see if I did trust God in death as well as life. I could live on to a ripe old age, and knit for my grandchildren. Looking back now, I realise that was not what Brother Tom told me. I was released from my *fear* of death only, and I was certainly released from that. 'Through his death he might destroy the Devil . . . and in this way set free those who were slaves all their lives because of their fear of death' (Heb. 2: 14–15).

Later that evening something else rather special happened. I suddenly found myself saying something that I had not thought out beforehand. It just came into my mind as I went along. I suppose it was a prophecy, but we usually left that kind of thing to Brother Tom! I wrote it down as soon as I got home. Because I wrote it at a time in my life when I was utterly happy and fulfilled – and yet it has such meaning for me in the light of what has happened since – I would like to copy it down here:

February 1982

    I am training a special people to be my companions throughout eternity, to be my heart's delight and joy. You will be able to praise and worship me so easily when you see me face to face, but I need you to learn how to do it now, down here. I do not want automatic praise which costs nothing. I want you to learn to praise me when you are depressed, downtrodden, being tempted or not having your prayers answered. That is when your praise and worship mean something to me. Learn it now, it will matter in eternity. I did not promise you ease and comfort. Remember that the more difficulties you have now, the more real Heaven will become to you. All I want is to live in you and use your body, personality and circumstances to show my reality and power.

I did not realise that night that God was gently and kindly trying to prepare me for what was to come; almost to explain His reasons for allowing it. I tucked the piece of paper away in a drawer where it lay forgotten for two years. It did not seem significant to me then. I was not 'depressed or downtrodden' and life was fun. I could not see why things could not be pleasant down here *and* in Heaven. Surely a God of Love could arrange that. If only I had stuck that paper up on the wall I could have saved myself so many hours of doubt and misery and God Himself the pain of my misunderstanding Him.

By the following Thursday, I had gone down with a violent attack of flu. Well, not exactly 'gone down with' because mothers of six children are so important that they never 'go down with' anything – or so I thought. If I had possessed a thermometer it would probably have registered around 104 degrees, but no way was I going to miss a precious Thursday House Group meeting. Anyway it was the only time in the week when Tony and I went out, just the two of us. I did feel a bit guilty spreading all my germs round that precious little collection of people, so I sucked antiseptic sweets, and sat as far away as possible from old Mrs Burton. But my conscience pricked me so badly that when Brian, our pastor, broke into a time of prayer by saying, 'I feel there is someone here who needs prayer for healing,' I did not want to admit to having flu. Anyway, I hate the embarrassment of 'being prayed for' in public.

But my sneezes and coughs gave me away and soon Brother Tom and Dr Jordan were firmly laying hands on me. I actually felt my body temperature dropping, and even my streaming nose dried up.

How wonderfully powerful God is, I thought. He said we could pick up snakes without being bitten, and we don't even have to suffer flu.

I felt so well I stayed up half the night! But the next morning I felt dreadful. I had read enough books on healing to know that when you have been prayed for, you *are* healed even if the symptoms still remain.

I must *hold on to my healing*, I told myself firmly as I went down to cook the breakfast bacon. This is only a test of faith. I only *feel* ill – really I'm living in health.

All that day I stalked round the house confessing that I was well. I had just read the book by Dr Paul Yongai Cho, *The Fourth Dimension*. What you say with your lips becomes a reality in your life. However by teatime I felt awful and my faith (and temper) were failing badly.

As I perched on the side of the bath watching Richard (four) and Duncan (six) splashing happily in the steam and bubbles I felt still more confused. Tony and I had come to believe firmly in the supernatural power of God to heal the sick. As Duncan sailed his boat round the treacherous waters of the bath, I remembered that it was only a miracle of healing that had saved his life five years before when the doctors could do no more for him. When you see something like that in your own family experience you cannot possibly doubt the reality of it. Yes, we knew then, and we know now, that God still heals.

At that time I was also convinced that it is never God's will for one of His children to be ill, yet that flu just would not go away. The sore throat stayed for three months. My arms and legs ached incessantly and became increasingly weak, while the pain in my head and eyes spread down my neck and spine.

'I am well, I am well, I am well!' I repeated as the Easter holidays arrived. I so love having the children and all their friends around the place, and the time of year is so busy in the garden, that there is just no time to be ill. It never entered my head to go to the doctor. Tony and I didn't bother much about illness; we thought that if you pretend you are not ill, you find one day that you aren't any more. Anyway, I was quite sure that most of the ill people I knew were only hypochondriacs wanting extra attention.

It was not that we disapproved of doctors. It was just that we were such an irritatingly healthy family, we rarely needed one, and believing in God's gift of healing I should have felt like a hypocrite dashing to the doctor before I had given God time to work. So instead of a visit to the surgery I steeped myself in tapes and books on healing.

When I became so giddy that I began falling flat on my face, the children thought it was a huge joke.

'Don't you dare tell Daddy about this,' I would say firmly, knowing that if he guessed how ill I really felt he would probably ring the doctor at once. Tony is a marvellously tolerant man and very easy to live with because he never seems to notice things. I'm sure that if I dyed my hair pink he would make no comment!

'Christians do not need to have problems,' boomed a well-known preacher's voice from my cassette player, as I struggled to wash up the dishes. 'Jesus said we could remove mountains by faith. The problems in our lives can seem like mountains, but we can all be problem-free people, perpetually living life to the full.' A cup fell from my hand, which was beginning to feel oddly numb, and shattered on the kitchen floor. 'Where am I going wrong?' I sniffed, as I fumbled awkwardly to pick up the pieces.

When Eunja came over for coffee I unleashed all my confusion upon her.

'You're doing too much,' she said in her forthright way,

'being a Sunday school teacher and dashing round speaking at coffee mornings. Why don't you just settle down and enjoy being a mother, instead of using up your energy doing Christian work outside the family? While they are so young they must be your number-one spiritual responsibility, so enjoy them – you'll only have them for such a short time.'

Perhaps she was right, but if that was all God wanted me to do, why did I have this burning desire to tell people about Jesus, and do some great work for Him? Could He not give me the supernatural energy to do both jobs? But soon I began to realise that I was becoming too ill to do either!

As I attacked the tide mark round the bath one morning, I experienced a devastating feeling of panic as I realised my body was just not under my control any longer. At that 'happy' moment the door bell rang – it was Rosemary from up the lane, a leading light in the local Red Cross. She watched in silence as I struggled to make us some coffee and then demanded, 'Why for Pete's sake don't you go to the doctor?'

'I don't like to bother him,' I protested. 'Anyway, I had a lifetime's share of the medical profession when I was younger.' Pride (and I believe it was pride by this time) comes before a fall, and as I jumped up to answer the phone the vertigo was so severe I fell flat on my nose at her feet.

'That does it!' she said indignantly. 'I'm coming tomorrow morning to take you up to the surgery.'

I knew I was very ill by then and needed proper help quickly, but I still felt God wanted to heal me without bothering the National Health Service. So when Tony came home I said, 'You know that bit in James 5 about he that is sick calling the elders to pray for him?'

'Yes,' answered Tony from behind the *Daily Telegraph*.

'Well,' I continued, 'do you think you could ask Brian,' – our Pastor – 'to pop round and pray for me? I haven't felt really well for months.' The *Telegraph* collapsed like the walls of Jericho. After years of being surrounded by so many children and so much activity, we had almost lost the art of talking to one another and we were certainly both ostriches when it came to ignoring anything unpleasant.

'Why ever didn't you tell me?' he enquired. 'I'll go and ring him at once.'

But Brian was in London and his wife promised he'd come the following evening. Next morning in the doctor's waiting room, I really did feel I was going to waste his time. I was so totally convinced that when Brian came everything would be all right, that when the doctor told me to go straight home to bed and not to move until he came to see me the following day, I felt a terrible fraud. Brian was coming that evening, so I'd probably be out digging the garden when the doctor arrived.

But Brian did not come. He was unavoidably detained in London and rang to say he'd come the following morning. None of us knew there was any need for urgency. I also believe that God actually prevented him from coming at that stage. It's as if God sometimes allows things to get worse for His own purposes, which we can't understand at the time. When Jesus took so long to reach Bethany in John 11, was it so that a greater miracle might be done?

That last evening that I was to have at home for so many months has lodged in my mind like a video recording. Naomi, who was then nine, and Richard cuddled into my bed and I read aloud *Rainbow Garden* by Patricia St John. Something odd was happening to my speech, and I sounded as if I had drunk several glasses of whisky. But they did not seem to mind, and I felt Richard's little warm body relax as he fell asleep in mid-chapter. Duncan, a hyperactive six-year-old, was far from warm and cuddly, and insisted on using my bed as a trampoline. At last my head would stand it no longer, and Sarah, our eldest daughter who at fourteen was very much my deputy, marched him firmly off to bed. At ten o'clock our son Justyn, then thirteen, padded into my room with the portable television. The Falklands war was at its height, and he and I had watched every news bulletin, but with a great feeling of guilt because Tony is a pacifist and did not approve of our patriotic fervour.

In the middle of the night the pain in my head and spine was so appalling I could not keep it from Tony any longer.

'I think you've got encephalitis again,' he said, and his voice sounded strange and thin through the darkness. I realised suddenly that it had not only been pride or faith which had delayed my visit to the doctor. It was buried fear. All the strange sensations I had been experiencing were not new to me. They were like the repeat of a horror film I had seen nearly twenty years before.

## Chapter Two


Tony and I first met in the early sixties through my father. He was Tom Rees, and he worked full time as an evangelist, travelling around the country telling people about God. At that time the Beatles and the Rolling Stones were at their height, and my younger brother Justyn was 'Stonestruck', and had just bought himself an electric guitar. He had a good singing voice and began to compose his own songs about God which he and I used to sing together raucously while we helped with the washing up.

'Why don't you two form a group to sing at the young people's rallies in the winter?' Father suggested. Not a very revolutionary idea you might think in these days when guitars are almost as common in churches as organs are. It wasn't like that twenty-five years ago. After our first performance in the City Temple Church, Holborn, Father received shoals of letters from shocked Christians, outraged by the sacrilege.

'It would not have been so bad,' wrote one vicar's wife, 'if they had used wooden guitars, but all those wires and amplifiers!' The drums were too shocking for her even to mention.

Father was a very wise man, and replied, 'We must move with the times. Young people today are far more likely to listen to someone telling them about God if they hold a guitar in their hands.'

There were six of us, five boys and me, and we called ourselves the Peacemakers. Tony was one of them, and it was a case of hate at first sight. We loathed each other.

Not all the Christian world disapproved of us, and although we were one of the first groups of its kind we were soon being asked all over the country to lead youth services, Christian Union meetings, Sunday school anniversaries and even weekend missions.

Our parents were both well-known preachers, and I'm sure Justyn and I only got the invitations because our name was also Rees. But we were painfully aware that the ability to speak in public is not necessarily handed on in our genes, and we were both shy, diffident people with no great personalities to project as our parents had. The group had been formed simply to accompany singing, but suddenly we found we were both expected to preach to packed churches or even town halls. We were scarcely out of our teens and both suffered from massive inferiority complexes, because we constantly compared ourselves to our gifted parents.

'I can't stand up in front of a church full of people and tell them about God,' I protested to the first vicar who had invited us to his church. 'I'm much too shy.'

'Just open your mouth, and let Him do the talking,' he replied simply.

That night was probably the most important of my whole life until then. I could feel God standing behind me using my voice to tell people that He loved them and wanted to make them happy and whole. I could see as I looked at their faces that they were responding to God. It was not me talking: I could feel the power of God surging through me. Labelled as 'backward' at school because of undiagnosed dyslexia, I had withdrawn into a private world of failure. Suddenly I realised that God did not only use superstars like my parents, he could even use *me*, and I knew that all I wanted to do for the rest of my life was to stand and watch God at work.

The three years that followed were the most hectically enjoyable years of our lives. We were all working or studying in the London area. Tony was at teacher training college, Justyn was doing hotel management, and I had a job in a nursery school. I can't think how they ever managed to pass any exams, because we met up most evenings to pray and practise and then set off every Friday afternoon to travel anywhere in the land, wedged into our ghastly old van between the amplifiers and drums.

Sometimes we slept on newspapers and other times we were entertained like royalty, but each weekend we saw God changing people's lives.

Tony and I argued and quarrelled all the way until we realised we could not manage without one another. It dawned on me that being a housewife and even a mother need not prevent me becoming what I most wanted to be – an evangelist.

Somehow, in all the happy rush of life, we never found time to buy an engagement ring. Then suddenly one evening when we were setting up our musical equipment the world began to swirl around me, and a few days later I was in the National Hospital with viral encephalitis.

Practically unable to speak, see or move I lay wondering how Tony would feel about me now. Many young men would have fled, but he strode firmly down the ward full of people in wheelchairs, and said, 'Until we manage to buy that engagement ring, I want you to keep this instead,' and taking the cuff link out of his shirt he put it into my hand, closing my limp fingers around it. If I lost my engagement ring today, I'd be quite cross, but if anything ever happened to that cuff link, I'd be heartbroken.

His love gave me the will to live and his encouragement helped me to fight the effects of the disease – which is an inflammation of the brain. It took two years of determined effort to get completely well, but finally we were married in 1966 and with our travelling days behind us we settled down to life in the Hertfordshire village of Sarratt. I shelved my ideas of becoming an evangelist, and tried to force myself into the mould of a perfect housewife.

'But you can't have encephalitis twice surely?' I protested, as I tried to make myself swallow the cup of tea Tony had kindly made me long before first light.

'Viruses can lie dormant in the body for years,' he replied gloomily, 'and then just flare up again. Look at your symptoms – they're much the same as last time.'

I'm not going to have encephalitis again, I told myself firmly. After all, the healing ministry was almost as unusual as guitars in those days. Brian had promised to call that morning, before going on holiday, so he just *had* to make it before the doctor. I felt it was my last chance, but the doctor came first, and I heard him and Tony making serious noises in the room below.

'We're getting you into hospital, Mrs Larcombe,' the doctor told me brightly. 'Just for some tests.'

'I know,' I replied crossly, 'a lumbar puncture, thanks for nothing.' He was a very nice man really. It was not his fault he was a doctor!

It was not a playgroup morning, and we felt Richard might be upset seeing me whisked away in an ambulance, so Tony took him off with him to work, and I felt quite alone and rather frightened as the ambulance lurched along the country lanes I loved so much. I had missed Brian by half an hour.

As the mother of so many energetic children, I had spent hours in the casualty department of the Kent and Sussex Hospital with endless scalds, cuts, broken bones and even a small tummy full of junior aspirin. But there were no long hours of queueing for me that day, and as I was whisked through the corridors on a trolley I thought how funny people looked upside down!

'You can always squeeze something to laugh at out of every situation,' my grandmother used to tell me, but as I was abandoned in a lonely little cubicle to wait for the doctor, my sense of humour deserted me. I cursed myself for forgetting to pull something out of the freezer for the children's tea, and remembering that the first thing they all do as they come in is shout 'Mum!' I wondered how they would feel when they got no reply.

'Lord, let them remember You're there with them,' I

implored, 'and help me to do the same.' Suddenly that tiny room was totally full of His presence. It was as if He took the whole load of all my worries and poured His peace into the hole where they had been. I lay there smiling up at Him – positively basking in His nearness.

Opening my eyes suddenly, I saw looking down at me the most beautiful pair of grey eyes I have ever seen. They seemed to be floating above a medical white coat, but surely no one with a smile like that could possibly be a doctor! He was Polish, and even if I could remember his name I would never be able to spell it. It took hours to piece together my medical history, but he never became impatient when I got muddled or ran out of breath. He was just about the only doctor I had ever known who treated me like a sane human being, and explained what he was doing as he examined me. Finally he sat down beside me and said, rather as one might discuss the weather, 'I think you have an inflammation of the brain, and the fluid round it, which goes down your spinal column. I think the casings of your nerves are also inflamed, and the lining of your heart, and you have probably got some clots in your lungs. Does all that worry you?'

I am quite sure it would have, before God had cushioned me with that supernatural peace. Many people had told me before about that special grace He gives His children in sudden crises, but He never gives it in advance, so we only fully believe it as we experience it. He had taken away my worries so I could quite genuinely reply, 'No, I'm not frightened at all, because I am sure God knows what He's doing.'

He leant forward, suddenly interested. 'You believe in God then?' he asked almost wistfully.

'Oh yes,' I replied. 'What about you?'

'I did once, and I loved Him deeply – my parents are devout Catholics, but since I began my medical training I've seen so much suffering, I don't feel so sure any more.

'Anyway,' he continued, standing up rather suddenly,

'We've got plenty of time to talk about that later. I'm sending you up to the ward now, and when I've had my tea, I'll come and give you a lumbar puncture.'

I knew from bitter experience that having a needle stuck into your spine to tap the spinal fluid is not a pleasant experience, but that lumbar puncture was almost enjoyable compared to the first one, many years before, because that young doctor just could not stop talking about God – quite regardless of the two nurses who were assisting him.

'What possible reason could God have for letting you be here like this, with all those children at home missing you?' he demanded as he stuck extravagant quantities of sticking plaster all over my back.

'I don't know yet,' I replied with as much dignity as someone in that position could muster. 'But I'll tell you when we meet in Heaven.'

It was supposed to be a feeble attempt at a joke, but he stood looking down at me very searchingly before he said, 'Lie flat and don't move for twenty-four hours,' and he was off down the ward, leaving me with nothing to do but to pray for him.

Naturally Tony could not come and see me that night, he was far too busy putting everyone to bed, but the Lord sent me the only other person I really wanted to see just then – my brother Justyn. I nearly died of surprise when he appeared beside my bed. I had not expected to see him again for years. He was just leaving to take on a church in Canada, and we had said our tearful goodbyes some days before. Within two minutes of his arrival he had me laughing and he had brought me something very precious: a card from our cousin Max Sinclair.

A few years before, Max had broken his neck in a car crash, and had spent many weary months in Stoke Mandeville patiently regaining some use of his limbs. Justyn read me what he had written: 'Sue and I just want you to know we're praying for you. We know only *too well* what you and Tony are going through just now. The next seven days are going to be tough, but here's a verse to help you through. We've broken it down into a tiny phrase for each day.

> 'Fear thou not
> For I am with thee
> Be not afraid
> for I am thy God
> I will help thee
> yea I will uphold thee
> with the right hand of my righteousness
> > (Isa. 41: 10 AV).'

I got through the next week simply by repeating the tiny phrase for each day, over and over again. I was far too ill to cope with long passages of scripture or even whole verses, but I could cling to three or four words. How well Max understood that.

After Justyn had gone, I lay holding the little card for a long time, thinking about Max, and a great feeling of shame spread over me. Clearly I remember the day he had his accident, and we heard he was completely paralysed. How angry I had been! We were on holiday in Devon and I had stamped up and down the cliff tops raging at God. How could He let a thing like that happen to Max who had given up his career to serve the Lord full time at Hildenborough Hall? 'What a useless waste!' I stormed.

But it had not been a waste, and I realised how much more God had been able to use Max since his accident. Because he knows what it feels like to suffer, people with many kinds of problems feel they can trust him, and when he tells them about Jesus they listen in a way they might never have done when he was fit and healthy. His love and prayers meant so much to me that night simply because he did understand.

'Sorry, Lord,' I whispered, and I wish I could say that I drifted peacefully off to sleep. But pain in my head and back reached a terrifying level, and I bit my tongue so hard it bled. Across the ward a woman was having a violent attack of asthma and making a great deal of fuss. None of the nurses took any notice, probably for some very good reason, but it seemed to me quite useless to ask for help, as no one would care.

'Lord, send someone to help me!' I pleaded. In my semi-conscious state I had no idea of the time, but when it seemed like the middle of the night, I suddenly found the Polish doctor standing by my bed.

'I thought you might be feeling a bit uncomfortable,' he smiled.

'How did you know?' I asked.

'God must have told me.' Was he mocking me? I didn't really care, for my opinion of doctors reached an all-time high as he stuck a needle full of heroin and morphine into my arm.

Next day, I think I must have been much worse. They moved me into a darkened side ward because I could not stand any light, movement or sound. The next thing I remember is a night nurse trying to make me drink some tea out of a cup with a plastic spout, and saying brightly, 'It's Sunday morning.' Sunday meant church to me, and I felt so lonely for all our Christian friends. Then I remembered that hospitals have chaplains who bring round communion. That would be so lovely, but he would probably only go into the main ward. He would never find me in this dark little cupboard. Desperately I prayed, 'Lord please work a miracle, let the chaplain come in here.'

I had hardly finished praying that when a very dear and familiar face floated over my bed. Of course! George Swannell who had been our friend for many years was chaplain of the Kent and Sussex! He is more like Jesus than any other man I know; in fact during muddled moments during the next few weeks, I often mistook him for Jesus himself as he sat by my bed, sometimes for hours on end.

His view of illness was quite different from many of my friends'. He was often quoting Samuel Rutherford, who lived some three hundred years ago and did not seem to feel that illness was a sin or a work of Satan when he said, 'Blessed is the fever that fetcheth Christ to the bedside.'

Christ certainly came to my bedside that Sunday morning, wearing George's body.

It must be terribly easy to think that people who look unconscious cannot actually hear what is going on around them. Actually they can, and I am sure I heard far more than people intended I should. Over the next week the virus that was causing the inflammation was gradually winning, as one by one my body's systems went out of action. Tubes were pushed into all kinds of embarrassing places. My arms and legs wouldn't go where I wanted to put them, and I couldn't see because the darkened room spun round. Soon I began to have difficulty in swallowing even soup and fruit juice through the plastic spouts. I kept forgetting how to breathe and gasped in terror like a fish on a marble slab. They put cot sides up round my bed because of convulsions, and I was convinced they piled goats, geese and turkeys into this 'cage' with me. In spite of these hallucinations, part of my brain remained totally clear and alert to everything and everyone around me. I was literally hanging on until Brian came back from holiday. Then I knew all would be well.

## Chapter Three

In comparison with what Tony was going through, I was having a holiday. It is always far harder to watch the illness of someone you love than to be ill yourself. He longed to be with me, and I needed him, but he had the awesome responsibility of so many children. He did not go to work for the first week, and he also had the support of my brother and his wife Joy who, bless them, delayed their flight to Canada.

But he had to make plans for rather a bleak future. His job as a teacher adviser not only takes him to schools all over Kent, but also to places as far away as Devon and Scotland. He needed reliable cover for his absences. Countless people offered to take some or all the children off his hands, but he had been a teacher long enough to know that children cope better in a crisis in their own familiar surroundings and routine. He tried to be father and mother rolled into one, as well as visiting me, so he constantly felt torn in two, and the phone never stopped ringing.

Naturally my friends and relations wanted a daily progress report and they wanted to talk to Tony himself. It was only their loving concern which prompted them to ring, but every time a bedtime story reached its climax or the fish fingers went into the pan, the phone rang, and Tony had to go over the same depressing details which lowered his spirits a notch every time.

Many people rang to say, 'Tell us what we can do to help.' How often I have done that in the past. But Tony was suffering from shock and he says his mind just used to blank out. He knew he needed help badly, but he just could not think what help to ask for. 'Well, just ring when you think of something,' people would say. Strangely, when you are in the middle of a crisis you hardly ever do that. You either feel you will be a burden or you are so paralysed by shock you cannot pluck up the mental energy.

Everyone reacts differently to stress. Some people need friends around them all the time, and constant phone calls reassure them, while others can only cope in privacy. Tony is the private sort. Our little church longed to surround him by physical and tangible expressions of their love and concern, but he just could not bring himself to go to church. The singing and sympathy made him feel emotional. I was visited by one well-meaning lady weeks later who said, 'What a pity your husband has lost his faith, we haven't seen him in church since you left home.'

Actually Tony's faith deepened and matured greatly, but he needed to be left alone. Perhaps we expect other people to react to a crisis in the way we would ourselves, and it is easy to be baffled, hurt or even shocked when they seem to need a different kind of help. I am sure the Lord can and does give us wisdom to know what people need when we ask Him specifically.

Tony became more and more independent, and sensing people's disapproval, he withdrew further and further into his shell. The friends who helped him the most were the ones who just did things without being asked. For many weeks Grace, a busy house mistress at a nearby boarding school, 'broke' into our house each morning and scooped up from the floors, beds and drawers all the dirty washing, returning it next day, washed, ironed and prayed over. Several people deposited whole meals on the doorstep, foil-wrapped and complete with vegetables and gravy; such a lovely change from fish fingers! Some people would arrive unexpectedly and take the children off for a picnic or a trip to the sea. If they had rung the day before, the children, who had become rather clingy, might not have been brave enough to commit themselves.

Poor Tony also had to cope with Janie who reacted to my absence by rejecting him utterly, and withdrawing from the family into her own little icy world. She would not even address a remark to him and would say, 'Sarah, will you ask Dad to pass me the salt?' Many men would have been baffled and frustrated by that, but Tony realised that Janie had been hurt too many times, and was just protecting herself from future pain.

Tony longed to shield the children from as much suffering as possible, so he did not tell them how ill I really was. Recently both the two older ones, Sarah and Justyn, told me how angry and hurt they felt because of that.

'Dad just kept saying, "Mum's fine, everything's all right," but we could feel he was keeping things from us,' said Justyn, while Sarah commented, 'If only Dad had got us all together and told us straight out every single thing we would have felt safer and been able to help him more.'

It is so easy to look back and think what people should or should not have done. When you are drowning, you have to keep swimming hard and there is no time to think about psychology. Perhaps Richard and Janie could not have coped with straight talking like that, even if the others would have felt happier knowing the truth. Probably children are like adults and only the Lord can show us how to treat them in the individual way that they each need.

When I had been in hospital for just over a week I discovered a very important doctor hanging over the side of my cot. I guessed he must be important because he wasn't wearing a white coat!

'We've decided to move you to a hospital in London, Mrs Larcombe,' he shouted. (Why do they always shout? Just because a person is ill or foreign does not mean he is deaf!) 'They have more advanced equipment up there,' he added.

'All right,' I grunted. 'But get this goat off my legs.' He turned and said something to Sister that I was never intended to hear: 'We're probably too late to move this one,' and for the first time since Brother Tom's pronouncement in

February, I remembered I was supposed to be going to die. But I had been definitely released from the fear of death, and I felt nothing but joy at the prospect.

All that day I felt life slipping away behind me, rather as the land recedes when you float out to sea in a boat. But there was something I knew I had to do urgently. Tony must not feel guilty about marrying again, but when he came to visit me I was not brave enough to bring up the subject. So, with the help of a friend I wrote that pre-planned letter to him, and gave it to George, saying, 'I'm off to Heaven, can you give this to Tony when I get there?'

'I certainly will!' he replied with a beaming smile. How often we can rob people of the joy of looking forward to Heaven. George looked really pleased for me, but he told me weeks later that the letter felt like lead in his pocket for days.

They gave me a nurse all to myself that day, and Sister and the Polish doctor seemed to be constantly in the room. I felt so safe and cared for, the last thing I wanted was a trip to London the next day. The pain was so ghastly that even the thought of moving was terrible and to leave my dark room and face the daylight would be shattering. I profoundly hoped I would die in the night! But long after visiting time was over, suddenly there was Brian with his wife Penny. They had dashed home from their holiday, straight to the hospital. Sister herself showed them in; I suppose she thought they had come to bring the last rites!

'I'm going to Heaven,' I managed to say.

'We know that,' Brian replied gently, 'but we've come to pray for you. I'm not sure how to pray, so I'm just going to start, and see what happens.'

I still don't know how he prayed; all I could hear was his voice as he and Penny sat either side of my cage holding my hands through the bars. His voice grew fainter and fainter as I began to have difficulty in breathing.

So this is what dying is like, I thought as I began to float above the bed. The pain was stopping at last, and suddenly over my left foot at the end of the bed a soft gentle light began to glow. I knew it could not be in the room because it did not hurt my eyes – nothing hurt any more. It was the entrance to Heaven, and I could not wait to get inside! God was there waiting for me, and any minute now I would see Him face to face. And then He spoke to me.

'What do you want me to do for you, Jen?' This was not quite what I had expected. Before me lay all the freedom and glory of Heaven, the Lord Himself, and so many other people I loved. Back down in the darkness behind me was pain and discomfort.

'I'm too tired to choose, Lord,' I said fretfully. But He seemed to be waiting, and through the darkness I saw Tony and the children standing in a little group.

'Well,' I said rather ungraciously, 'if you're giving me the choice, I suppose I had better go back to be with them.'

Very gently, He said, 'Very well, from this moment you will begin to go back. It is going to be a struggle, *but I will give you my strength.*'

Suddenly I could hear Brian's voice again still praying on, and I interrupted him rather rudely.

'It's all right now, you can stop praying. It's all been done, I'm healed.'

'Amen,' finished Brian hurriedly, and they kissed me good night and went home. Later that week I dictated a description of all that happened that night to my friend Rhoda and months later I stuck it into my black book.

How wonderful that Brian had been prevented from coming until I had been allowed the privilege of looking right into Heaven. I know now that I shall never again be afraid of dying – it is the loveliest thing that can happen to a Christian: total, utter and complete healing.

When Brian and Penny had gone, I felt desolated. Heaven never seemed further away. I was convinced that God had healed me, but the pain was back, and tomorrow was only a few hours away. If the healing was not going to be instant I felt I would rather not have had it at all.

It might just have been the hallucinations, but I felt

36

horribly conscious of the powers of evil that night. They seemed to surround my cot – above me and below, angry, menacing, vengeful. Wherever was God, I wondered, as I lay shaking in terror. Suddenly a white shape loomed over the bars. It seemed to have no head, but it spoke to me.

'Mrs Larcombe, are you afraid?'

'Yes, very,' I squeaked, 'but you can't hurt me, I belong to Jesus.'

'That's great, so do I!' and a large, strong and very human hand gripped mine. The dim light from the porthole in the door revealed that the apparition was only a white coat worn by a very tall black man.

'My name is Mr Jones, and I am the Senior Nursing Officer,' he told me. 'I am in charge of this hospital tonight, and I came to tell you I shall be taking special care of you. As I walk round the wards and corridors, I want you to remember I shall be praying for you, all through the night.'

I shall never know if it was the beginning of the healing process or Mr Jones's prayers, but I never had another hallucination – no, not one single goat. Just when I thought God had deserted me, He sent along one of His most special servants to reassure me.

Long before the night staff went off duty, Tony crept unnoticed into my room. He had not been able to sleep either, and had spent the time digging around in Philippians.

'Look what I've found!' he said gleefully. It had blessed him so much that he had decided to make the twenty-mile round trip to Tunbridge Wells to share it with me before the children woke up. 'For you have been given the privilege of serving Christ, not only by believing in Him, but also by suffering for Him . . . Your life in Christ makes you strong – that's your bit, Jen, and this bit's for me – and his love comforts you' (Phil. 1: 29, 2: 1).

'We've had such fun serving the Lord together, haven't we?' he went on. 'In the Peacemakers, at church and with the children. All that was so much easier than serving Him in this way, but it's just as important to Him.'

37

Of course I could not read the verses he was showing me, but he underlined them so hard in my Good News Bible I can't miss them now. We held hands, and thanked God together for these lovely little gifts to us both.

'Serving Him has been fun,' I said as he sat quietly beside me. 'But *knowing* Him is more important. I wish I knew Him better.' That sent Tony rummaging further into Philippians 3: 10: 'All I want is to know Christ and to experience the power of His resurrection and to share in his sufferings.'

I did not have much breath, and words were still very hard to bring out, but I told Tony as best I could that the evening before I had really experienced the power of His resurrection. But we could not understand what sharing in His suffering really meant. Later that day I began to understand.

Before he left Tony gave me a pair of extra-dark glasses to help me through the journey, then the door swung closed behind him as he dashed home to get the children up and off to school. But I really did not have time to miss him, I was so completely surrounded by love and care. My own nurse gave me an extra-special blanket bath and packed my few belongings into a grey polythene bag.

'Don't worry about the journey,' she said. 'I'll be coming in the ambulance with you.'

The Polish doctor came in, full of enthusiasm for the visit to this country of the Pope, which was just finishing. Not only had it inspired his Roman Catholicism, but it had restored his faith in Jesus Christ.

'Don't worry about the journey,' he said. 'I've laid on a special modern ambulance for you – so smooth you won't know you're moving.'

I had to laugh when Sister came in at that moment and said, 'Don't worry about the journey, I'm going to give you a huge injection just before you leave.'

I was so spoilt and cosseted, I never realised it was going to be the worst day of my life.

# Chapter Four

The neurological department of the large teaching hospital where I was taken is famous throughout the world for its high standards, but everyone can have an off day, and I just happened to arrive on one of them. The ward was divided into glass cubicles, and the first thing I remember was piercing light attacking me from all four sides at once. My own nurse was gone and in her place, writing at a small table, sat a female dragon in a white doctor's coat.

'Please,' I whispered hoarsely, 'would you mind drawing the curtains?'

'No,' she replied shortly, 'I have a great many notes to make and I can't write in the dark.' I thanked God for the small help of Tony's dark glasses and gritted my teeth.

'Come along now, Mrs Larcombe, wake up!' she rasped in a hectoring tone, 'we've got work to do.' The Polish doctor had asked me all the same questions but had left me still feeling like a human being. After an hour with her, I was reduced to the status of an imbecile animal. She bullied, shouted and banged the table in exasperation when I got muddled over the dates of my pregnancies – even in full health it's hard to remember so many! The more she cross-examined and accused the more stupid I became, as I tried to keep telling myself she must have had a row with her boyfriend or been on duty far too long. But over the next few days I heard her shouting at elderly and often simple-minded patients, some of whom were immigrants with very little English, so perhaps it was just her particular bedside manner.

'I am going to examine you now,' she said. 'So take off those ridiculous glasses and open your eyes when I'm talking to you.' Sister had packed my ears that morning with wads of cotton wool to keep out the pain of sound, but with a revolted snort she pulled them out and threw them on to the floor.

'Follow this pin as I move it,' she shouted. But I could see two pins at least.

'How many fingers am I holding up?' I felt even she could not have eight on one hand! Then she discovered my plastered back.

'What sort of an imbecile put all this stuff on?' she roared, and as she ripped it off I felt like Poor Old Michael Finnigin in Richard's nursery rhyme book, who 'took off half a yard of skin (agin!)'. But when she finally tripped over my catheter bag, she really lost her cool.

'Staff Nurse!' she bellowed. 'Come and take this ridiculous thing out at once. Mrs Larcombe will use a bedpan or else . . .' The staff nurse – who I later learned was deeply concerned about this woman – replied coldly, 'Only the night staff remove catheters in this ward, Doctor.'

'Well, I've a good mind to yank it out myself,' she replied, and stormed off to Sister's office. I was told later in the week she had put her feet up on Sister's desk and said, 'Well, that one's for the cabbage patch for sure,' meaning I was so hopelessly brain damaged, I would never be any good again. It was only her first term in neurology, and how was she to know the Lord was beginning to heal me?

I sighed with relief, thinking she had gone for good, and it was then that I realised how wildly thirsty I was. I had been so frightened of being sick all over the ambulance that I had purposely not had anything to drink that day, and as swallowing had been difficult the day before, it was probably over twenty-four hours since I had had a sip of any liquid. Suddenly my tormentor was back.

'They are ready for you in the EEG department, so we're sending you straight down there for an electroencephalogram.

After that you'll go straight for a brain scan and then a chest X-ray.'

'Please,' I begged, 'could I have a drink of water first?' She looked annoyed and glanced at my locker. 'They haven't been round with the water jugs yet,' she snapped, 'and we can't keep the technicians waiting. They're very busy, so you'll have to wait.'

I managed to make no comment, but then to my horror I saw a wheelchair being pushed through the door. When you have done nothing but lie completely flat and still for nearly two weeks, even sitting in a comfortable armchair for a few minutes is a great shock to the system, but this was no comfortable armchair! The steel back bit into my painful spine and there was nothing to support my head which lolled about ridiculously.

'Please,' I begged, 'couldn't I go on a trolley?'

'Trolleys take two porters,' she replied firmly, 'and we're very busy today. But we'll send a nurse with you.' The nurse was male and looked very bad-tempered.

All this sounds as if I am grumbling horribly, but actually I learnt more of the pure love of God that terrible day than I had done in thirty-nine years before it, and I could not have learnt some of those lessons any other way.

As we rocketed off down the corridors, up ramps and round corners, the severe vertigo made me feel I was on a speeded-up version of the looping star at Margate fun fair! The pain in my head and spine was quite terrifying, while behind me the porter and nurse chatted away to each other amicably. Had they understood what vertigo is like, they would have supported my flopping head or at least put a hand on my shoulder.

I became aware of someone screaming like an animal in a trap, and was deeply humiliated to discover it was me, who had always prided myself on having five babies without a whiff of gas and air! The men behind me were laughing; I am sure it was at some joke they were sharing, but I felt they were mocking me in my humiliation. Then suddenly before

41

my tightly closed eyes I saw Jesus. He was hanging on the cross. *He* felt totally humiliated as well, mocked by uncaring professionals, hurt by the utter indifference that allowed them to sit and watch Him there (Matt. 27: 36). For the first time ever I realised a tiny fragment of His awful pain, and yes, human terror. I knew He understood just how I felt. He was right there with me in it, minding for me and hurting with me. Then it dawned on me suddenly that He had gone through His worst hours separated from the comfort of His Father's presence, utterly forsaken and alone, because He was not only being punished for my sins, but was actually being blamed for them, and all because He loved me so much.

But *we* never have to face anything this life can throw at us, without His presence and support. When we are really suffering physically or through bereavement, rejection or loss, it does not help to think of Jesus sitting in triumphant ease, enthroned in Heaven. It can almost feel as if He watches us writhe and squirm while going through the nasty trials He has planned to test our faith and build our spiritual character.

'Seeing' Him there on the cross at one of the most horrible moments of my life showed me that when we suffer, He suffers too. Nothing happens to us that does not deeply affect Him as well. It is not just that He remembers His own sufferings – He *feels* ours with us. When we are Christians He lives in our human bodies (I Cor. 6: 19). So naturally He feels every pain and grief with us because we are part of Him, and (incredible thought!) He is part of us.

Naturally I did not think all that out clearly at the time; I was hardly in a fit state for deep theological thoughts! But I have been convinced ever since that because He is so near us in our blackest times, one of the greatest of all the sufferings of the Lord Jesus must be to see people He loves reject Him and turn away from Him when they are hurting and needing Him most.

I can laugh now (but I couldn't then) at the very ordinary

prayer that I uttered at such a sublime moment in my life. As I realised I was going to faint and fall forwards out of the wheelchair (pulling all my tubes with me) all I could say to the Lord was, 'Please don't let me lose Tony's sun glasses.' They had become to me then what his cuff link had been nearly twenty years before.

When I came round, crowds of people seemed to be milling around far above my head, poking oxygen masks, stethoscopes and needles at me, while an authoritative voice thundered, 'A patient in this condition should never have been in a wheelchair; fetch a trolley at once.' I had a fleeting glimpse of my male nurse looking crosser than ever. And my dark glasses were gone.

The next thing I clearly remember is lying on a narrow bench having the electrodes glued to my head for the EEG. I had had one nearly twenty years before, so I knew they were quite painless, except for the horrid bit at the end when they flash lights into your eyes to measure how quickly your brain reacts. It was so lovely lying still at last, I might have been happy if I had not felt so thirsty. The technician sat behind a glass partition, but I was conscious of not being alone. Somewhere to my right, I felt the glowering morose presence of the male nurse. During a break in the proceedings, I plucked up all my courage and asked him for a drink of water.

'They don't have any down here,' he snapped. 'Wait until you get back to the ward.'

That could be hours, there were still the brain scan and X-rays. What a perfectly horrid young man! I thought. He shouldn't be a nurse at all! Hating him took my mind off the thirst quite marvellously, but then to my dismay I discovered God had another lesson for me to learn that day. (Life with Him is not always pleasant but it is never boring!) Suddenly I 'saw' the cruel callous soldiers hammering nails into those kind work-worn hands that had never been used for anything but good. How desperate would have been their punishment in eternity for such bestial cruelty, if Jesus had not prayed,

43

'Father forgive them, they know not what they do.' That same Jesus had said earlier, 'Pray for them which despitefully use you' (Matt. 5: 44 AV). He practised what He preached.

'No, Lord, that's going too far,' I said firmly. 'Why should I pray for this vile young man who laughed at me, let me fall out of a wheelchair and can't even be bothered to get me a drink?'

'But he needs you to pray for him.' So (very crossly) I gave in and began to pray, and almost at once I *knew* why he was in such a bad mood. Without really thinking what I was doing I said to him, 'You're very worried about something, aren't you?' He had been slouching in the chair, his head down on his chest, hands deep in the pockets of his white overall, but when I spoke he sat upright, like a puppet jerked by strings.

'How did you know that?' he demanded.

'Well,' I replied nervously, 'God just told me while I was praying for you.' He almost sprang across the room towards me, pouring out a great torrent of words. He *was* desperately worried and frightened about something that was going to happen to him the following day, and he was almost crying as he told me all about it.

'Do you really believe in prayer?' he finished at last.

'Yes, I really do,' I gasped. 'I'll pray for you specially tomorrow, and I *know* God will help you, to prove just how much He cares about you.' As I drifted off into another faint, I remember saying to the Lord, 'I'm trusting You for a miracle – it's Your honour that's at stake.'

High above my head I could see water. A whole cool jug of it. Was it another hallucination, I wondered. No, I was back in the ward, brain scans and X-rays just a dim nightmare I had slept through. The jug stood on the high locker beside my bed. The late afternoon sun blazed at me through the wall which was one huge window, and my glasses were gone. Could it really only have been that morning Tony had given them to me? What a whole world away Tony seemed. My thirst was urgent now; I had to have a drink. But even the male nurse seemed to have gone off duty, and I was far too weak to lift a glass, let alone that jug, even if I could have reached it.

'I'll suck my flannel,' I thought, not caring how soapy it might be. Then I saw my grey bag of possessions far across the other side of the room. Even if they had not had time to unpack it, they might at least have left it within reach. I was much too frightened to ring a bell, even if I found one. Never have I felt so alone, and broken in my life. 'This is a God-forsaken hole,' I muttered. Then a wonderful thing happened. In a hopeless gesture of defeat, my hand flopped against the side of the locker and hit something metal. I did not have much feeling in my fingers, but I knew there was some kind of bracket there. With quite indescribable joy, I realised it contained a little Gideon New Testament. Some Christian member of the Gideon Society had taken the trouble to place it there, and had probably prayed for everyone who would lie in that bed. I fumbled it out of its brass pocket and fell asleep holding it in my arms. I could never have read it, but it represented a tangible proof of the presence of God there with me. I wonder how many other desperate people in prisons, hotels and hospitals throughout the country have been blessed by those Bibles, as I was that day. Above all, it taught me that there is no such thing as a God-forsaken hole.

Some time during that evening I remembered a sermon I had once heard, and had thought was rather silly! The preacher had said that thirst must have been the worst part of the cross for Jesus; the heat of the sun, the salty taste of blood and each breath a gasping effort. When he said, 'I thirst,' it was not like the fretful complaint of a feverish child, but a desperate, agonising need – he was dehydrating.

You have to experience real thirst before it is possible to know how horrible it is. All that I experienced then was only a minor pin-prick in comparision to all His suffering for me, but in my comfortable, protected, happy life I had never really suffered anything. Before that day Jesus had been someone to be served, followed and prayed to, but I never really *knew* Him until I could identify with Him in His humiliation and pain, discovering also that He was identifying with me.

His suffering was voluntary; I had no choice. At any time He had the power to stop that pain, and summon legions of angels to scorch off the face of the earth all the people who hurt Him, mocked Him or ignored Him. Only His faithful steadfast love for me, and sinners like me, kept Him there to the bitter thirsty end.

## Chapter Five

Not often in a lifetime is one woken first thing in the morning by a stark-naked man doing a war dance round the bed! It was my first experience of being in a modern mixed ward, and it certainly made a change from goats and geese. He was hustled away by two sweating night nurses and I later learnt that the poor man had a brain tumour. When he had gone, I could not help wondering what else might befall me that day.

I need not have worried. Sister returned from her holiday and all the confusion of the previous day was forgotten, as she unleashed upon the ward the highest possible standards of care. I was not even allowed to sit up in bed and went for further tests on a trolley. Under her efficiency the world felt safe again, and all the scowling nurses started smiling while their cockney wit was better than any medicine. Even the 'mocking' porter of the day before padded into my room with my sun glasses, which he had found under a radiator. How good the Lord is to care so much about little things. He *did* work a miracle for that male nurse, and we became such good friends, he even brought his wife and baby to wave at me through the glass wall on his day off.

My feelings about mixed wards were – mixed! It is hard enough trying to use a bedpan without being held on one by a man, and when the nice old chap next door died and was rolled away in a huge metal box on wheels by two hilarious porters just before lunch, I secretly hoped he might be replaced by a nice, fully clad female.

But it was not a feminine face that I saw beaming at me through the glass when I woke from an afternoon nap. That man just has to be a Christian, I thought. The same idea occurred to him as he saw my Bible lying on the still impossibly high locker. He pointed to it, waved and positively jumped up and down with excitement. However, the beginning of a promising conversation was firmly nipped in the bud by the appearance on his side of the glass of the Female Dragon to take his case history. His face looked like a pricked balloon as it disappeared suddenly from view.

Much later in the evening he paid me a proper visit, looking subdued but not entirely crushed. He had recently had a wonderful new experience of God, after having attended the same very dull church all his life. He was now 'Heaven bent' on turning the whole place upside down, and said with shining eyes, 'Things are really happening now in our church – I never knew being a Christian was supposed to be such fun!' It was so kind of the Lord to bring him with his infectious joy and exuberance.

I told no one about that first terrible day in London (Tony might have been arrested for woman slaughter if I had!) because the next day the Lord told me very definitely that I had to forgive, as an act of will, everyone who had made it so unpleasant, and you cannot forgive unless you also try to forget. That sounds a bit odd when I have written it all down like this, but I learnt so much from that day, it would be less than honest to leave anything out. It was perfectly easy to forgive the porter and male nurse, but every time I heard the rasp of the doctor's voice down the passage, I broke into a cold sweat, and I still have nightmares about her now. Forgiving seems to be impossible for me without God's help, so I started praying for her every day. I think it must be working, because I can laugh about her now, even if my subconscious is still sweating!

The first experience of that glass cubicle might have been hellish but the rest of the time I spent there was nearer to

48

Heaven than I thought it possible to be while still earth-bound. Justyn brought me a present of a personal stereo so I could listen to tapes of hymns and Christian songs through the earphones. I could not read, but God just reached into my soul through the music. I lay there basking in the presence of God.

I had been brought up in an age when the emphasis was on serving God. Every ounce of strength and each moment of time must go into working for Him. 'Let go and let God' was a scornful way to describe a lazy Christian. Then the worship explosion had hit the church and I found that new and refreshing. It was great to feel all the inhibitions going as the wonderful new church music bathed my soul.

But I could never get away from a deep feeling of doubt. Was this more active form of worship really coming from inside me, or was it something I was supposed to do because everyone else did? Was it becoming just another liturgy most of the time?

What I was experiencing there in hospital was something quite different. It was the source of a river bubbling out of me to meet with God; it was not something I was working up or putting on. I could not have stopped it if I had tried.

It cured one secret fear that I have always had. Being such an active person, I have always had a sneaking feeling I might get terribly bored in Heaven, but I realised once and for all in that cubicle, that eternity itself will not be long enough to enjoy the full loveliness of God.

The news from Tony was better. Mrs Ashman, a Christian friend in the village who had run the playgroup where our children had been so happy, offered to be a stand-in mum for several days a week. Dear old Gom, my old nanny, promised another day a week, and Richard was happy to stay with a friend on the remaining day. He has nothing but happy memories of those months, due, I am sure, to so much prayer and the kindness of Christian people.

But my deep mother-hen instinct needed to be *doing*

49

something for my children, so I felt I should be praying for them. Strangely that is very hard to do when you are ill. People say, 'Aren't you lucky having all that time to lie in bed and read the Bible and pray?' But you cannot concentrate. First I felt guilty about it, then I used to imagine taking each one by the hand in turn, and leading them to the throne of God. I did this frequently throughout the day, watching the clock for their 'vulnerable' times – the hassle of getting off in the morning, dinner break at school, coming home to no mum, and bedtimes. It was such a lovely peaceful wordless way of praying, but some days when the pain was very bad, I could not even manage that much. Then I would just say, 'You pray for them, Jesus.' 'He ever liveth to make intercession' (Heb. 7: 25 AV).

The first Sunday that I was in London, a very wonderful thing happened to me. The chaplain came and gave me communion about eleven in the morning during a gigantic thunderstorm. When he had gone, I was quite overcome by the joy of the Lord. What I did not realise was that all over the country and even across the Atlantic congregations of Christians were praying for me in their Sunday services. How good of them. Mostly they did not even know me, but I have had the privilege of meeting some of them since. As they closed ranks, I was wafted up on the strength of their prayer.

Poor old Eunja, and a friend of hers called Gill, had been fasting for days ever since Eunja heard I was in hospital. She told me she felt personally responsible! That Sunday the Lord told her to stop – all was well.

As I lay there I had a vision. I know it was not just another hallucination like the goats, because it later came true. Rhoda came to see me that afternoon and I got her to write it down for me, and it is now pinned into my black book.

I saw God as a tall strong father striding through a deep dark valley. The rocky walls were so high they almost blocked out the sky. Behind huge menacing boulders lurked evil monsters, waiting for a chance to grab me, but I was perfectly safe, because God was carrying me. I looked like I did when I was about two, golden curls and a pink smocked dress. My chubby arms were round His neck and we were talking and laughing happily together. Green slimy rocks were under His feet, but He never stumbled or dropped me. We were utterly enjoying each other. Then suddenly we came to a small sinister valley leading off the one we were in, and at the entrance stood Satan, mocking me.

'She's just loving all this attention you're giving her,' he sneered. 'You're making it too easy, send her down this valley alone. It's called depression. If she can't feel your presence she'll soon lose her faith.'

The one thing I have always feared is depression. I believe it is the worst thing a human being can go through.

'Lord,' I implored, 'I'll take any amount of pain or disablement, so long as I feel You with me, but please – not depression.'

He looked down at me so kindly and said, 'We must prove Satan is wrong, just as I had to with Job. I will *always* be with you even if you cannot feel Me. I have promised My presence with you for ever, but I never promised you would feel it. Your trust in Me will never grow in a perpetual state of joyous feelings. It *is* going to be a dark valley. But I will be there even if you don't *believe* it.'

I had to struggle very hard to accept this, and when at last I did, I expected to go straight into a deep depression. But the God 'who will not let you be tempted beyond what you can bear' knew I was not ready for that experience yet (1 Cor. 10: 13 NIV).

## Chapter Six

When you are lying flat on your back alone all day, the truth about your damaged body does not really hit you. There is no one to see you or to compare yourself with. But when I was moved back to the Kent and Sussex Hospital into a general medical ward, I became acutely conscious that I was a physical wreck. My arms and legs were impossible to control and they twitched and shook, while my eyes blinked and winked embarrassingly. When the physios came round and tried to stand me upright, the vertigo crashed me to the floor.

I hated the humiliation of wheelchairs. Have you ever realised that when you are in a wheelchair you are not considered a person by most people? No one ever addresses a remark to you, they only talk to the person pushing you! I was determined to lurch and reel around the ward on my own, however silly I looked, but I had to travel down to the physio department each day in a chair. To discover that you cannot control your body is an enormous shock to the system, but the Lord was good enough to meet me even in that.

One Sunday morning George came into the ward for early communion. I had made an awful fool of myself by falling over in the loo just before, and was still shaking from shock and rage. But as he handed me the wafer dipped in the wine he said (quoting Jesus of course), 'This is my body, broken for you.' I felt the tears of joy trickling from the corners of my eyes as I inwardly replied, 'and this is my body broken for you, Lord. Paul said, present your bodies, as a living sacrifice (Rom. 12: 1 RSV), so here you are, have mine.'

I could not think what He could possibly want with a broken, twitching body like mine, but I felt unutterable joy in giving Him something even as useless as that. However, as the days went by I have to admit I often felt it can be much harder to be a living sacrifice than a dead one.

Being ill gives you an entirely different perspective on life. I found myself noticing things much more and becoming acutely aware of how people react. It was as if my own suffering had given me an insight into other people's.

I learnt how small things can so easily increase an ill person's misery; things that I had done without thinking in the past. I was determined that I was going to learn from having been on the receiving end.

Lying watching other patients with their visitors showed me how people so often pretend to be better than they really are so that friends and relations don't go away feeling miserable. I saw patients lie quite still and quiet all day until their visitors arrived. Then they sat up and laughed, talked and generally put on a good impression, only to collapse with exhaustion when the bell was rung to clear the ward.

Visitors, however lovely, are a strain. When people come from a long distance they feel they must stay as long as possible. A three-hour visit is probably fine if you only have a broken leg, but when you have been very ill your span of concentration is only about five or ten minutes at the very most. The worst thing of all is having several people who don't know each other sitting on different sides of the bed. The effort of communication with them all, while turning your dizzy head from one side to the other, is devastating. One at a time and never for more than a few minutes, is going to be my future rule when any friend of mine is ill.

Tony and I are devoted to one another, but we are very different. I needed my friends round me, and their love carried me through and reassured me I was still a person. But it was hard on Tony, who is a very private person. Sometimes he just longed to have me to himself to let off steam about the children, but he could not get near the bed for people who were too insensitive to see his needs and leave us alone together.

We very carefully planned Richard's first visit to me one afternoon, and I had lots of little parcels ready under the bed clothes for him to find and a story to pretend to read from a book. That first meeting was crucial if we were to begin to rebuild our relationship after so many weeks. But no sooner had he settled down and begun to relax slightly, than three visitors arrived. Tony tried to explain to them, but they irately said they had come a long way, and had another train to catch, and surely Richard could come any time. Richard could not tolerate my divided attention and behaved so badly Tony had to remove him in haste, leaving me to the visitors and a lump in my throat the size of a turkey egg. Tony never risked bringing him again, but my yearning for him was a physical pain.

Visitors brought me so much wonderful fruit that if I had eaten it all I would never have left the loo, and the boxes of chocolates were gorgeous, but not much use when I was too nauseated to manage more than dry bread! I liked best the visitors who said, 'I haven't brought you a present, but when I come next time what would you like me to bring?' The nail file or envelopes you really need are worth all the exotic presents you are too ill to appreciate.

It is lovely when a visitor reads a verse from the Bible, but better still if they also write it out on a card so if you have failed to concentrate at the time you have it to chew over later. Short, quiet prayers are wonderful, but when visitors kneel down, or worse still raise their arms in loud praise, it is rather difficult to live in the ward after they have gone home!

It is also desperately embarrassing when visitors break ward rules and insist on coming out of visiting hours. One friend of mine was always turning up in the morning. She managed to time her visit to coincide with Sister's coffee break and she strode confidently in remarking to anyone who

54

noticed her that she was a *hospital visitor*! They must have thought she was some kind of a social worker, for she always got away with it.

There is always a very quiet patch in a ward between the violent activities of bed-making and washes, and the serving of lunch and pills. It was into this deathly hush that my friend always insisted on reading several long chapters from obscure parts of the Old Testament in a very loud penetrating voice. But it was worse still when she began to pray for me and my very personal needs, while the whole ward listened in – eyes popping with interest!

The best hospital visitors are people who have been very ill themselves, but not the ones who make your stomach turn by a recital of the horrors they suffered, or encourage self-pity by getting you to talk about your own. You just want to be treated like a person again, but some people cannot help talking to the handicapped in an odd voice reserved also for small children and imbeciles.

I received many letters while I was in hospital and my reactions to these also changed my preconceptions about how an ill person can be best helped. All the letters were well-intentioned and full of sympathy, but some were so gloomily spiritual that I felt more in need of comfort at the end than I had before I started reading! Illness, like bereavement, can make people extraordinarily sensitive to tactless comments. It was very hard for people to get it right!

This was never the case with the letters I had from my mother's youngest sister, Geraldine. She seemed to know instinctively how I was feeling but never probed or patronised. Instead she told me all the funny things that kept happening in the remote Scottish village where she lived, recounting them so vividly that I would cry with laughter. She wrote frequently, on a battered old typewriter, and I would re-read the letters over and over again. Through Auntie Gerry's letters I rediscovered the humour in everyday happenings, as I started looking out for funny things to tell

55

her. The joy of the Lord started becoming a positive thing again; I was no longer just getting through the day but relearning to enjoy the small things that make up life.

Occasionally she would write about spiritual things, but she did so by way of discussion – sharing her own thoughts and inviting my response. She didn't write in the sort of charismatic or evangelical language that so many Christians slip into without realising, but in a direct and personal way which didn't give me that horrid feeling of always being on the receiving end. It was exactly the sort of help I needed; profound and yet practical.

Then there were the healers. Naturally the Christians who came to see me prayed I would get better, but sometimes people would come with a strong burden to lay hands on me. That was lovely, but I felt convinced I *had* been wonderfully healed, and I accepted the healing was going to be a slow and gradual process. I felt I should only be thanking God for what He *was* doing.

'But it is *never* God's will for us to be ill even for one minute,' said one earnest friend. 'You must be harbouring some secret, unconfessed sin, or you could walk out of here now.'

All that night I could not sleep, as I went back over a lifetime that seemed to contain nothing but sin. By the time the early tea came round, I had reached the conclusion that if God was punishing me for all or any of that, it was a wonder I was not in the hospital mortuary!

That afternoon, after a long hard session in physio, when the only thing that had kept me going was my desire to get better quickly to see my children again, it was rather lowering to be told by another visitor, 'Your trouble is, you're just accepting this, and not fighting. Satan has possessed your will.'

George told me that as a hospital chaplain he sees some Christians who expect God to heal them instantly, and when He does not, their faith is shaken. So they lose the comfort He longs to give them and they blame themselves. The resulting guilt and depression rob them of their natural human will to fight their diseases, so they are hurt spiritually, mentally and physically. Fortunately for me, I had the memory of looking right into Heaven and I clung to the certainty that I had been healed.

Guilt is a weapon Satan can use very easily in illness. Endless people said, 'You brought all this on yourself, you know, you've been doing far too much.' I have heard that said so often to people who have had heart attacks, strokes or nervous breakdowns, but what is done is done, and piling guilt on top of suffering does not help.

Having said all that, it is vital to add that the love and company of all those visitors really gave me the will to fight back towards the real world. Hospital visiting is one of the most special jobs a Christian can do.

I realised how much I was helped by them all when after a few weeks back at the Kent and Sussex, I was isolated again in the side ward. A bad relapse and a complication of the disease had set in.

## Chapter Seven

I was utterly shattered. Where was the healing God had promised me? Or had He promised it at all? Had He just given me back my life and told me it would be a struggle? The pain was sometimes worse than I felt it was possible to live through; I felt angry and desperate.

Suddenly the double swing doors of my cubicle were thrust open and in strode the neurologist from London. I peered at him in terror, fearing he had brought his assistant with him – but fortunately he was alone. He came over and stood looking kindly down at me.

'Well, Mrs Larcombe,' he said, 'they tell me you have developed complications.' I apologised profusely and assured him I had worked extremely hard at my physio.

'Much too hard, I'm afraid,' he smiled. 'You want to run before you can walk.'

He produced the inevitable red-headed pin that all neurologists wear in their lapels like a badge of high office, and proceeded to stick it into every part of my body. I didn't mind at all; I couldn't really feel it because my skin had begun to feel like the thick hide of a hippopotamus.

'Can you smell this?' he asked, producing a tiny bottle from his pouch. I had to admit I could not even smell the gorgeous flowers that filled my room or taste my toothpaste. He seemed quite put out when he could not reduce me to helpless giggles by scratching the soles of my feet and when he had done all the things neurologists always do, he sat down on the end of my bed.

'We must have a little talk, Mrs Larcombe. What seems

58

to be happening is that the inflammation is now damaging the actual nerve casings, so that messages from your brain are taking longer to reach other parts of your body. That's why you have to concentrate so hard even to manage small simple actions. The nerves that affect your heart, breathing mechanism and temperature control are all affected. You see double and your eyes hurt because of damage to the optic nerve, and you feel seasick and giddy because the nerve controlling the body's balancing mechanism is faulty.'

'How long will it be until the inflammation dies down again?' I asked.

'We just don't know that,' he replied while his kindly smile slipped away. 'You must face the fact that you might be left permanently damaged.'

'You mean I'm not going to get completely better,' I faltered.

He did not answer, but turned away and did something that I had no idea important consultants would ever demean themselves by doing. He bent down and pulled my bedsocks back on!

'Rest,' he said quietly, 'that's the best thing you can do,' and the swing doors of my room flapped shut behind him.

Rest! For me that was a rude four-letter word. I lay and gazed bleakly at the wall. Had I really understood what he was trying to say? What was that going to mean to the life I had so carefully organised for myself?

I longed to talk to Tony about it, but when he came to see me that night he looked completely exhausted – drained of all strength like someone who has had a haemorrhage. I wondered if Sister had told him what the neurologist had said; somehow I just could not bring up the subject. If he looked that bad when I had only been ill for a few months, how could he face living with a permanently disabled wife – no longer attractive or able to cope at home? Would he go on loving me?

For the next three nights I had a recurring dream. I had always lost something and was desperately, hopelessly searching for it. I wondered if I was mourning the loss of my own body and strength. Our whole happy lifestyle was threatened. We could not go on living deep in the country if I could not drive the children to all the places they needed to go. What about the home-made bread and cooking our home-grown vegetables? A handicapped mum could never run that house and garden, and if I could not walk into the woods and fields, how could I escape from the pressures of life at home to communicate with God? I really panicked, and all that fretting and churning gave me such severe headaches, I felt life was intolerable.

I decided to have a talk to George about it all, and I had plenty of time to do so because he came every single day. When the pain was at its worst, he just sat and held my hand like my father always did when I was ill as a child. The test of a real friend is when you *don't* have to talk and silence is relaxing and not awkward. I sensed he understood completely how I was feeling, but he cared too much for me to soothe me with trite words of sugary sympathy. Instinctively he realised the danger I was in, and firmly pointed out the trap that self-pity and doubt can be.

'I think our old enemy Satan is having a go at you,' he told me. 'Why not use your sword and fight back?'

'Sword?' I faltered.

'The sword of the Spirit which is the word of God' (Eph. 6: 17). 'If I give you a verse, do you think you could go on repeating it to the Lord, to yourself and to Satan until I come back later?'

How much I gained through his spiritual discernment. So often our Christian friends just rub us with soothing ointment, when really we need spiritual castor oil! George gave me Romans 8, from verses 31 and 32: 'If God is for us, who can be against us – He gave us His son, will He not also freely give us all things?'

I felt such a fool repeating that over and over again, and old Satan sat on the end of my bed and laughed at me.

'I'm still fighting,' I told George weakly when his head popped round the door later in the afternoon.

'Keep it up!' he said. 'Maureen (his wife) and I are really praying you through this.'

It was late in the evening and that horrid time of the day in hospital when you long for sleep, but have to force yourself to stay awake for the sleeping-pill trolley to come round! I was still 'doing my homework' and wondering why the Lord was not dealing with Satan, when it suddenly and finally dawned on me: *God was for me!* So Satan could *not* prevail against me. God was not going to deal with Satan *for* me. He had delegated that authority to me. 'Resist Satan and he will flee from you' (James 4: 7 RSV). So I told him firmly in the name of Jesus to go, and he did!

As well as giving me Jesus, God was going to freely give me all things. I nearly shouted with the joy of it. Did the 'all things' mean healing, or courage and endurance to cope with a new life, and could not the God who made everything in the world be trusted to take care of one man and six children?

I was so excited and released, no amount of sleeping pills acted on me that night. About three in the morning I was listening to some riotous choruses on my headphones, but what I did not realise was that I was singing loudly along with the tape. I could not hear myself, but suddenly an enraged night nurse burst in.

'What do you think you're doing?' she demanded. 'You'll wake the whole ward.' Even my embarrassment could not spoil my joy, and later that night, or probably the next morning, I was conscious of Jesus sitting at the end of the bed, where I had felt Satan to be, so recently.

'What is it that you really want me to do for you?' He asked. I was overcome with a deep sense of awe and also a certainty that this was one of the most important moments in my life. My first instinct was to say, 'Heal me, Lord, and I'll walk right home.' But I waited a moment to give myself time to think. I felt His power was so present, I must not bungle this precious interview with the King of all Kings. What *did* I really want most? Well, I am a mother, so it was obvious.

'Lord,' I replied at last, 'most of all I want *all* my children to grow up to know, love and serve You, and marry people who love You too.' He seemed to be waiting, so I dared to add, 'Please give Tony a massive dose of Your strength and blessing, I love him so much.'

'And what about *you*?' He said at last. 'What shall I do for you?'

If He had asked me that nearly twenty years before, or even twenty months, I would have replied, 'Lord, let me do something really big and important to serve you.' But something had changed inside me, and it was unthinkable that I should just go back to being the same person I had always been before. This deep worship relationship with Him had become so precious to me that I really did not care what else life held or did not hold for me, so long as I could keep that.

'Lord,' I began rather diffidently, 'I've always had this hang-up about worshipping You. I've put on worship like a Sunday hat for church or House Group, but it's been so different here in hospital. Please couldn't I spend the rest of my life worshipping You day and night like Anna the prophetess in Luke 2: 36? Please give me a continuous secret relationship with You – like Brother Tom has.'

Now here I have to confess something, because I am writing this in the presence of God. I did not ask for bodily healing, because I was convinced He would heal me anyway! After all, the Lord asked Solomon what he wanted and when he asked for wisdom rather than riches, the Lord was so pleased with him, he gave him both! I thought the same rule would apply to me!

I drifted happily off to sleep, and in the morning I might well have been tempted to think the whole thing was just a dream, if the Lord had not given me a very special proof of its reality.

On the very day that George and Maureen were so specially praying for me, a farmer's wife in the back woods of Somerset pulled on her wellingtons and splashed down the muddy farm track to post a letter in the box half hidden by the overgrown hedge.

Peggy Darch had known God all her life, but recently her relationship with Him had 'come alive' in a new way, and she found He was giving her the gift of composing spiritual poetry as she helped her husband Ken with their dairy herd or made the clotted cream. The letter she posted reached me that morning, and here is an extract from it.

'Some weeks ago, the Lord gave me a poem – not one bit of it is for me, but I suddenly felt I should send it to you:'

> I am with you in the pain
>   I am with you in the sorrow.
> In the heartache of today
>   and all that comes tomorrow,
> I will never leave you.
>   I have promised to be near,
> so lift up your head rejoicing,
>   be delivered from your fear.
>
> I will hold you close beside me
>   as we walk along together.
> Take my hand and dance along
>   in the sun or stormy weather.
> Do not ever let a cloud or fear
>   fall across your lovely face,
> for I've made you to be beautiful
>   and I've done it all in grace.
>
> I love you dear to walk with me,
>   your company is sweet.
> I love your quiet listening
>   when sitting at my feet.
> Please do not feel inferior,
>   I love to hear you sing.
> Stay close beside me always,
>   my dear daughter of the King.

Peggy knew nothing of how I was feeling when she wrote that, and only God's perfect timing could have caused her to post it on just the right day. As I lay there clutching it that morning, I knew it was a tangible confirmation of all that had happened in the night.

One morning a few days after this, the ward domestic came into my room at 7.30 to mop the floor as usual. She had to do it three times every day, once with a dry mop, once with a wet one and once, I believe, just for luck! Her cheerful, uncomplicated friendship meant a very great deal to me, but that morning she was looking far from cheerful and her huge round face was all blotchy with tears.

'What's up?' I asked. Dropping her mop, she plonked her enormous bulk down on the end of my bed.

'Do you believe dreams mean anything?' she began. I grinned ruefully and said I was beginning to think that they did.

'I lost my dad a few months back,' she continued, 'and last night I went and dreamt I saw him in Heaven.'

'But surely that was a very nice dream, wasn't it?' I asked, puzzled.

'You don't understand,' she wailed, as the tears trickled down her round cheeks. 'That means I'll never see him again, and I loved my dad.'

'But why will you never see him again?' I insisted.

'Don't tell anyone, will you,' she pleaded with a sniff, 'but I just can't help shoplifting – oh, I've never been caught,' she added fiercely, 'but God wouldn't have a shoplifter in Heaven, so you see I never will see my dad again, will I?'

I fumbled into my locker for a tissue for her, and prayed hard for wisdom. She blew her nose and went on rather shyly, 'I felt you were the kind of person who might know how I get to Heaven.'

'I *do* know how you can get to Heaven,' I said, praying Sister would not look through the glass porthole in the door. 'And what's more, there'll be lots of shoplifters up there, and murderers as well.'

Her eyes opened in amazement.

'I thought only good people got to Heaven,' she said.

'No,' I replied, 'only bad people who admit they're bad and ask Jesus to come into their lives and change them.'

'Is that *all* I've got to do?' she asked, as a great beam spread across her face. 'Don't I have to get the vicar to do a special service for me in church?'

'Well, you can if you like,' I replied, 'or we could talk to the hospital chaplain about it, but there is nothing to stop you doing it right here and now.'

'I will!' she said. 'Before Sister catches me.' We shut our eyes and prayed together surrounded by her mops and buckets. I told George all about her when he came in, and later that day he talked to her and gave her a copy of John's gospel and some simple notes to help.

About a year afterwards, I was shuffling painfully through Tunbridge Wells feeling rather low, when something huge hurled itself at me from behind. It was my friend, the ward domestic.

'I've so wanted to see you again,' she beamed, positively jumping with excitement. 'I wanted you to know I've left the Kent and Sussex, and me and my husband are in Hailsham now, but we go to church every Sunday, and the vicar's so lovely, and,' she added, suddenly dropping her voice to a confidential whisper, 'I've never pinched another thing since I had that dream and learnt the way to Heaven.'

## Chapter Eight

'I'll go mad if I don't get out of this place soon,' I sniffed, as I hid in the loo for some privacy. I had reached a point where the hospital could really do no more for me, apart from providing rest, painkillers and physiotherapy. I longed to go home, but the doctors were adamant that I needed at least two more months of total rest.

'What you need is a good dose of Burrswood,' said Marilyn, an old school friend of mine, when she came to visit me later that day. Marilyn was the very first person I ever led to the Lord, and I still feel weepy now, thirty years later, at the memory of the joy of it. We were sitting up in bed having a midnight feast one summer holiday, when she was staying with us, and she asked Jesus into her life between two chocolate biscuits! Now she was the housekeeper at Burrswood, a beautiful country house set in magnificent gardens.

It was founded by a remarkable woman called Dorothy Kerrin. When God gave her a gift of healing, she opened Burrswood as a nursing home where religion and medicine could work hand in hand to care for and heal the whole person – body, mind and soul.

It is strangely moving to see the chaplain and the doctor working together in the services of healing in the beautiful chapel. For many of us who live in the district, Burrswood has become a place where we can retreat from the world for an hour or even a day, just to sit in the garden or pray in the chapel. There is a sense of the Lord's presence that seems to hover over the place. I could not think of anywhere, except home, where I would rather go.

I do not know who paid my fees for all those weeks, and I am still too embarrassed and grateful to enquire, but the afternoon I arrived at Burrswood, I really felt I must certainly have made it to Heaven this time.

Dorothy Kerrin believed people mend best amongst beauty and comfort, so the house is furnished exquisitely with antiques and restful colours, while quantities of flowers fill and surround the place.

Marilyn pushed my wheelchair into the most luxurious bedroom I have ever had, and produced a tray of china tea served in delicate cups. As I sat in my comfortable chair looking over the gardens, I felt all the bustle and pressure of the busy ward receding like a nightmare. However well run hospitals are, they are very impersonal and so noisy that sleep is almost impossible. Nor can you ever be perfectly sure that someone is not going to come at you with a needle or 'tear you off a strip' for not moving your bowels for ten days! I sat and cried for at least an hour just with sheer relief.

But after a few days of wallowing in luxury something rather odd began to happen. Everything was *too* comfortable and the staff were too loving. A terrible feeling of guilt set in.

Why should I be having all this lovely care while Tony and the children seemed to be going through hell? Everything was going wrong at home. Mrs Ashman's father had a stroke, so she could not help any more, the other friend who was looking after Richard had to stop because of a family crisis, and most other people had returned to their busy lives feeling, quite rightly, that Tony preferred to be independent. Even the social services were overloaded in that area and could offer no help.

Sarah had to stay at home from school for the last few weeks of term, and for a fourteen-year-old she did a remarkable job, but suddenly something broke inside her, and seeing no end to the tunnel of hard work, her anger and resentment against me, with its resulting guilt, boiled over and made her unco-operative and moody. She remembers actually wishing I had died. 'At least,' she said, 'we would have known where we were then.'

Jane's inner tensions made her unhelpful and withdrawn, but Duncan was worse than I dare describe him. Until I left in the ambulance, he had been quite an ordinary, lively six-year-old, but that summer his teacher at school told Tony she was completely baffled by his behaviour. He rudely rebuffed every overture of friendship anyone made towards him, and was so horribly naughty no one could possibly put up with him, except one very frail neighbour – Ann Frost, who, even though she was in constant pain from a disease of the spine, met him each day from school and let him lose himself in her garden until Tony came home from work. Poor Duncan, even the cat ate his beloved blue budgie.

Justyn was in very strict training for the National Swimming Championships. His training programme required Tony to do the twenty-mile round trip to the pool in Tunbridge Wells early each morning before getting the children's breakfast, then back to Tunbridge Wells and his office, home to get tea and put the younger children to bed, and finally back again to the pool with Justyn for a further session. The strain was almost too much, but he did not want to let Justyn down by failing to help him.

'Kind' friends came to see me and told me how appallingly Duncan was behaving and how worried they were that Tony was on the point of a breakdown. I could see for myself how exhausted he was, his mind and body totally overstretched. Then one day he dropped a bombshell on me.

'I've put the house on the market,' he said, 'and I've found us somewhere in Tunbridge Wells.'

I was completely horror-struck. I know I had been wondering how we would cope in Mayfield, but the actual realisation of leaving it was devastating, and surely it was unnecessary, because the Lord was healing me.

'Everything would be easier if we lived in town,' Tony claimed, but I wanted the security of my familiar and much-loved home, and the tranquillity of the country around me was a physical need. Even more, I felt I needed the people. In Mayfield I had an identity – I was a person

68

everyone knew. I did not believe I had the ability to make new relationships. Self-confidence is totally destroyed by a serious illness, and I felt I could not get better without the support of my loving Christian friends at church.

Of course I was being selfish – digging my toes into country soil. Tony, in his love for me, realised that I would not be the same person when I went home, and a new life would be less painful for me than discovering how much of my old life was now impossible. But I would not see it from his point of view.

'What about the children,' I stormed. 'They're insecure enough already without making them all change schools and church.'

I thought he was beyond thinking rationally, and he knew I was pig-headed! The last thing we both wanted to do was pray about it, but when at last we did, we settled on a compromise. We would leave the house on the estate agents' books until September, and then if it had not been sold by then, we would take it that the Lord wanted us to stay where we were.

But a horrid shadow lay between us, which did not help either of us. He became even more tense and strained, and something went wrong with my heart beat, so I had to be put on rather powerful drugs which gave me side effects and my physiotherapy had to be cut down.

As my anxiety about Tony and the children increased, I began to pray in an urgent, desperate fashion, but my prayers were becoming nothing more than an expression of worry – a faithless nagging at God, an endless repetition.

One morning as I sat in my wheelchair at the healing service, I felt God say to me, 'Lovest thou me more than these?' (Perhaps it's because I grew up with it that God often seems to speak to me in the Authorised Version.)

'What do you mean by "these" Lord?' I asked.

'Your house in the country,' He replied, 'do you rely on beauty and peace to feed your soul rather than Me alone? Your reputation in the village? Your status at the church? You enjoy people talking their problems over with you, it boosts your ego. Suppose I took everything away from you, would you still trust Me?'

I struggled like mad; He had broken my body, why did He demand everything else as well? I was sure Tony was wrong and I was right, but something inside me argued that if I really meant what I had said in the Kent and Sussex Hospital that night, that I only desired to worship the Lord and live in the sanctuary of Praise, it really did not matter where I lived or how few people I saw.

At Burrswood most people go up to the communion rail for the laying on of hands, but Father Keith Denerly always came first to those of us in wheelchairs. As he put his hands on my head that day, I offered my house, possessions, friends and psychological needs to the Lord, and asked Him to forgive and heal me from my pride and self-centred attitude. Afterwards I felt a lovely glowing feeling. I had reached a spiritual milestone – passed a test. I was to discover how wrong I was! If only we did not have to learn the same lesson so many times over!

That afternoon a kind friend brought Naomi over to visit me. Most people who brought the children to see me quite naturally stayed with us, but that made it hard for the children to relax and talk to me. This wise friend, Ann Frost, understood that and took herself off into the garden and Naomi and I were alone together for the first time since I had left home. As usual she set herself diligently to cheer me up, by telling me all the things that filled her nine-year-old world. She had won the silver cup at sports day, her mouse had nine more babies, and Mrs Frost's pond was full of baby frogs. But I could see she was struggling to fight back the tears, and was desperate not to let me see them.

'It's not right to bottle things up,' I said at last. 'Can't you tell me what's making you miserable? How is it at home?'

'It's fine really,' she replied with a gulp. 'It's just when we come home from school and no one's there to talk about the day.'

'But there's Daddy, surely?' I encouraged. She looked at me in helpless misery.

'Daddy's not quite all right at the moment,' she managed at last. 'He's all wound up like an alarm clock.' The tears were beginning to win and poor Naomi was panicking. If that dam burst she might never get back into control again. Just at the crucial moment, a glorious butterfly flapped in through the open window and rested on her shaky little hand. Naomi shares my deep love of country things, and it totally delighted us both by its utter perfection. No sooner had it flown away through the window, than we caught sight of a baby rabbit cheekily nibbling grass right by where we sat. We were so captivated we forgot to be sad, and Naomi whispered, 'Mum I think they were both really angels, sent to cheer us up.' Her calm was completely restored by the time she went home, and she looked quite supernaturally happy as she waved to me through the window. I believe angels can wear many disguises.

But I was in a turmoil that evening, terrified of what might happen if Tony cracked under the strain. What would happen to the children? I began my agitated anxious praying until someone knocked at my door. It was Father Keith himself. Spiritual counselling is as important at Burrswood as medical treatment. No one ever forces you into 'baring your soul' if you do not wish to, but there was the chaplain just when I needed him. God has never let me down.

'Oh, do please help me,' I pleaded, dissolving into tears. He slowly drew up a stool beside the comfortable armchair where I always sat overlooking the garden, and I was struck once again by the utter stillness of this man. He never moved a muscle as I told him of my concern and anxieties, and even confessed how I had concealed all my food in a polythene bag the day before so I could fast as well as pray. A crazy thing for a woman to do who had just rapidly lost four stone in weight. At last he said very gently, 'Naturally this illness is far harder for your husband than it is for you, and I think he and all your children need God's healing.'

'Yes of course,' I replied impatiently, 'but we'd never get them to a healing service – they'd never sit still long enough.'

'They don't have to come to a service,' he answered quietly. 'They can have the laying on of hands by proxy.' I was not perfectly sure what he meant, but he produced a little jar of consecrated oil from his pocket and said, 'Give me your hands.' Mystified, I watched as he rubbed the oil into my palms, but my mystification turned to horror when he knelt on the floor by my chair and bent his head.

'You lay hands on me,' he said, 'and I will represent Tony and the children.'

'I can't do that,' I protested, 'I haven't got a ministry of healing, and you're a priest.' He looked up and smiled at me.

'When I lay my hands on the heads of sick people, it isn't my hands that heal them, but the power of Jesus flowing through my hands. He can just as easily use your hands as mine. None of us are ever worthy to be used by God.' Then he bent his head again, and I had to get on with it. After I had prayed aloud and expressed everything to God we remained in silent prayer for a very long time – me leaning back on my pillows, and he kneeling motionless beside me. At last he said, 'I feel God has begun something special today, but you must leave Him to finish the job in His own way and His own time. He knows exactly what He's going to do and how He's going to do it. You have committed all your worries to Him; now by an act of the will you must leave Him to take care of them. These days we often demand instant healing from God, like instant coffee or mashed potato, but God's timing is perfect and He sees us from the other side of eternity where only the soul endures.'

When Tony next came to see me he was utterly different. He looked ten years younger.

'It's funny,' he said, 'but I feel I've been living in a nightmare recently, but it's suddenly beginning to lift, I can't think why.' I could think just why, but I did not dare to tell him, not just then.

The summer holidays were approaching – always a relief

for any teacher, but Tony had another problem to solve. We had planned our holiday that year back in January, long before the first rumblings of my illness. Through a Quaker friend, we had booked up to spend a week in a Quaker youth hostel in Yorkshire. My hopes of going with them had died long since, and Tony did not feel he could cope with a self-catering holiday all on his own. He was heartily sick of fish fingers. Then Ann Frost's daughter, Sarah, who was then eighteen and just about to go up to Oxford, offered to go with him and be a substitute mum. I wrote an urgent letter to our Sarah imploring her to see Dad had a real rest. She really took it to heart, bless her, and the two Sarahs firmly marched everyone off for long all-day rambles over the moors, disregarding Jane's grumbles and carrying Richard most of the way. That gave Tony time on his own with his Bible and the Lord to mend inside. He has never looked back since. How good the Lord is.

I thought I might feel rather flat with them all away on holiday without me, but it actually turned out to be one of the most eventful weeks of my life.

## Chapter Nine

'Have you ever heard that some physical illness can actually be caused by traumatic events in childhood or unresolved conflicts?'

Rosemary Anne, one of the Burrswood counsellors, had come to see me. I replied that I had never given it a thought, so she fixed me with her rather penetrating eye and said, 'Have you ever considered that you might need a form of treatment called the healing of the memories?' I couldn't help laughing.

'Not me,' I said, 'I had a wonderful and privileged childhood. Surely that kind of thing is only for people who've suffered horrible things.'

'I feel you should pray it over,' she said ominously. 'Lack of forgiveness and resentments can impede healing. I'll come back tomorrow.' As she went out of my room she turned, with her hand on the doorknob. 'We don't want to leave any stone unturned, do we?'

If I could have got better by turning every stone on Brighton Beach, I would willingly have done it, so if she was prepared to give a couple of hours of her valuable time each day, who was I to quibble? But I still felt a terrible fool, and dreaded her coming into my room for the first session. How could things that had happened to me years ago possibly be responsible for my succumbing to a virus? Anyway, I was embarrassed about letting another human being into the secret places of my life.

I need not have worried. During that week I often forgot

she was sitting there beside me. It was simply Jesus walking through my experiences with me, helping me to see people with His eyes, giving me the power to forgive, and also His forgiveness where it was needed. The complete atmosphere of other days surrounded me all the time, not just during the set times with Rosemary Anne. The smells, sights and feelings, things I thought I had totally forgotten, became more real than my bedroom. Gently my counsellor encouraged me to see Jesus in every event – actually to picture Him present. I realised He wanted me to be a whole person, with no hang-ups or chips on my shoulder. He needed to explain to me why certain things had happened, why people had acted as they did, and lovingly to show me where I had gone wrong.

The most exciting thing of all, however, was to see how He had actually healed me as I went along. I believe, after the experience of that week, that children from Christian homes, who are prayed for frequently, have a unique experience of being continually healed. They are not shielded from the traumas of life – in fact, they often seem to suffer more than most children – but if they are bathed in prayer, and are themselves willing, Jesus heals the wounds as they occur, and uses them for good. So although the concept of 'healing of memories' does sound a bit weird and way-out, it did teach me this wonderful truth of God's continuous healing for me all through my life.

It astounded me how fiercely we can relive past emotions. During the first session, I was quite overcome by a total feeling of rage. I saw the world through a red haze of hurt. I was three years old and being bathed by the new nanny. Suddenly I hated her so violently, I tore at her fat wet arms with my fingernails until her blood ran into my bath water.

'Oh God!' she screamed, flinging herself down on to the loo, 'help me to manage the dreadful child.' Then she burst into tears, but I did not care, and the next day I bit her.

My world had fallen apart, and I was bewildered and furious. My life had been spent in utter happiness in a tiny cottage in a country village. Father was away most of the time preaching, and Mother wrote books and painted pictures. She had a heart condition and was so totally undomesticated anyway, that Molly, a girl from the village, did everything for me. Together good old Molly (known as Gom) and I fed the chickens, pummelled pastry, and muddled along together. Mother was always there, and I could hear her typewriter clacking, even if I must not speak to her, and so break a mysterious thing called her chain of thought.

Then everything changed, it seemed to me, overnight. Through his huge campaigns in London, Father was leading hundreds of young people to God. In those days, just as the war was ending, regular church life had been disrupted; there were no cassettes, and few Christian books were being published. Nor were there any conference centres or great holiday celebrations as we know them today.

'It is not enough for people to turn to God, they must follow on to know the Lord.' That was the great burden both my parents shared, and it was then they received their vision of a peaceful country mansion – a centre for evangelism, teaching and rehabilitation.

That was why I was so cross. They exchanged our little cottage, climbing roses and all, for a huge dilapidated mausoleum surrounded by thirty-two acres of jungle that had once been a garden. Of course they could imagine how it was going to look, but I certainly could not. We arrived at Hildenborough Hall on a cold foggy day in November, and I trotted around the vast empty rooms, festooned with cobwebs, the walls crumbling with damp, while our few familiar pieces of furniture looked ridiculously tiny scattered around the neglected parquet floors. Father and Mother were naturally totally absorbed in materialising their vision, with the help of a willing army of (to me) strangers.

It might not have felt so desolate if I had still had Gom, but Mother was pregnant again, and it was felt that a real properly trained nanny should be engaged to take charge of me. Gom refused to desert me completely, and cooked for the community, but the terrible starchy creature who came to take her place did not like our relationship and established 'her' nursery in the old housekeeper's room behind the green baize door that had once separated the servants from the family. I was the wrong side of that door, and I could never find my parents when I needed them.

Gently Rosemary Anne brought me back to the present, praying for healing and forgiveness, and helping me to see those experiences from my parents' and Nanny's point of view.

'When our lives are shattered,' she said, 'as human beings we want to blame someone for it – ourselves, other people or God. When we blame ourselves we suffer guilt, and then often depression. If we blame other people, our personalities can be poisoned by resentment. If we blame God, we are worst off, because we cut ourselves off from our source of comfort and help.'

I blamed poor Nanny because really I knew my parents both loved me greatly, and minded about how I felt. They must have prayed a lot for me, and their prayers were answered, because I can clearly see now that three things happened to help me.

Justyn was the first. I know all the books would say that the arrival of a baby brother should have been the final end to my damaged security, but actually it was the beginning of my salvation. I loved Justyn from the moment I first saw him, and felt we were both in the same leaking boat together. All Nanny's crackling efficiency was unleashed upon his helpless body, and he was not even equipped with teeth to bite her! I was not alone any more.

Then, some time during that first year, I encountered God for the very first time. I must have become a terribly nervous child, and I was dreadfully frightened of the dark. The night nursery was down a long gloomy corridor and I was always terrified by the creaking noises the old wooden floors made as they contracted or expanded. One night I woke in a panic – I was sure I could hear footsteps creeping menacingly down

77

the parquet floor outside my room. I was paralysed with fear, too frightened to call out even if anyone would have heard me.

'God,' I pleaded, 'do something to help me.'

He did. Out in the garden beyond my curtains a bird began to sing. Then another joined in, two cuckoos held a conversation, and suddenly the whole world was full of wonderful music. I know now that it was only the dawn chorus, but I'd never heard it before, and felt God had put on a concert just for me. I remember feeling, as I listened in utter delight, that if God could do a miracle like that, just because I was frightened, then all I ever wanted to do in my life was to know Him better and better. He totally healed my fear, and I have never minded the dark since.

I suppose it must have been because of that desire to know Him that the other thing happened which finally transformed me into a happy child again. A lot of people don't believe children can, or should be encouraged to, commit themselves to God, to become indwelt by Him, until they are old enough to know exactly what they are doing. But when I was about four, I clearly remember sitting in a car in Jermyn Street in London with my mother. We were waiting for Father to see a man in an office, and I can recall so well the smell of the real leather seats of the old car, and see the feathery hat Mother was wearing. It was so lovely to have her to myself once again, that I asked her, 'Why do we have to live in that horrid big house with all those people?' (There were at least a hundred and twenty guests each week, plus a resident community of about thirty.)

'Because we want them to know Jesus, and ask Him into their hearts,' she replied simply.

'Why should they want to do that?' I persisted.

'Because Jesus can make them happy, and help them to be good.' Now I desperately wanted to be happy, and underneath my rages, I really did want to be good, so I asked her if I could do it too.

She could have said, 'Yes dear, when you are old enough

to grasp the whole concept of God.' But I desperately needed Jesus right then, and she understood that. I remember her praying a tiny prayer, which I repeated after her: 'Come into my heart, Lord Jesus, come in today, come in to stay, come into my heart, Lord Jesus,' and He did, right there in Jermyn Street.

It made a profound difference. I can see from old photos that my whole face changed from that day. I lost the frantic hunted look of anxiety, and became normal and smiling again, and I can remember myself the feeling of peace that stayed with me for days. I have seen the same thing happen so often with other troubled children. Once they open themselves up to God, He plants His own peace where there was fear, joy where there was hopeless depression, and self-control in very aggressive children.

Certainly I began to enjoy life from that time, and became excited by the miracle that was taking place around me. The house had been decorated before the first guests arrived, but it was the gardens that I really loved. I watched German prisoners of war dredging a bullrush swamp into a huge magical lake; ploughed fields were levelled back into the velvet lawns they had been before the war, and bramble thickets were discovered to contain rhododendron walks which I could easily imagine were fairyland. The resident community went into action producing their own vegetables, eggs and fruit, not to mention cream from Jersey cows, and I had the fascination of watching baby turkeys swelling into Christmas-plump gobblers. All this was very necessary in those days of ration books, when people had hardly seen cream or a freshly laid egg for years.

I also discovered that living in a busy community can feel very safe for a child. Whenever I could escape from Nanny there was always someone to talk to or watch. They were all working there because they loved God, whether they peeled potatoes or cooked them, made the beds or preached in the seminars. Father and Mother lived completely within the community, having only their bedroom and the study where

79

Father counselled people. Everyone had one single aim: to show the guests whom they served the pure love of Jesus.

Father and Mother both became spiritual superstars in their generation. Father filled the Royal Albert Hall more than fifty times and they both preached and broadcast all over the world. Through them I met many famous Christians. One of my favourite memories is of one day when I was out for a walk with Nanny and we met Father. He was deep in conversation with a young man in a real cowboy hat. 'This is Dr Billy Graham,' said Father, as I looked up into a pair of amazingly blue eyes. 'He has come over from America to help me tell people about Jesus.'

Of course I did sometimes resent the fact that my parents spent so long helping other people that they didn't have much time for us. But I think they must have realised that, because they both made a point of carving out time for us in their busy days. After lunch Nanny always took me to the study for half an hour with Father (or the Boss as everyone called him). Perhaps that was the only time I saw him, but during those thirty minutes he gave me his undivided attention and our relationship became one of the most wonderful things in my life.

Father always got up early to pray alone in his study, but Mother sat up in bed with her Bible on her lap and she never minded us snuggling in beside her. She never had to force us to have a time with God ourselves each day, we both just caught the habit.

She always sat in the nursery at meal times, telling us stories. She really made the Bible come alive, and Joseph, Moses and David were far more popular than Winnie the Pooh or Peter Rabbit.

I laughed ruefully as I thought of the hectic whirlwind our meal times are at home.

'I must be a terrible failure as a mother,' I told Rosemary Anne. 'But I suppose Mother did have Nanny there to shovel cereal into Justyn, and cut me toast soldiers. Nanny must have had some uses, but at the time I could never see any!'

Rosemary Anne and I had quite a bit of praying to do at the end of that first day's session. So much of Duncan's behaviour was now explained to me. Just as I had been angry with Nanny because she was not the person I had lost, so was he furious with everyone because they weren't his mum.

I had never accepted Nanny, and I must have made her life very hard. But I knew perfectly well that she disliked me as much as I hated her. 'But,' I finished, 'I suppose there is not much I can do about that now because she's dead.'

'But it's not too late,' said Rosemary Anne. She went on to explain that it is perfectly possible – and very necessary – to forgive and release people even after death.

When I reach Heaven I won't feel embarrassed about meeting poor old Nanny now, but I do wonder if she has forgiven *me* yet for spitting so often into her hat!

When we started the next day's adventure, I was almost suffocated by a devastating feeling of failure. I saw myself standing outside a huge white building – my school. I knew without a shadow of doubt that I could never go back inside it again. Human beings can only take a certain amount of humiliation before they crack, and I knew my cracking point had been reached.

Unfortunately for me, dyslexia had not then been widely recognised. I was just labelled as 'backward'. Everyone else in my class of eleven-year-olds could read perfectly, so why couldn't I? My mind was full of ideas and stories, but if I tried writing them down teachers fell about laughing at my spelling, and often shared the joke with my derisive class-mates. I might not have been so far behind them in subjects where dyslexia does not matter, if I had not spent every winter off school with pneumonia, rheumatic fever or bronchitis. I had no friends at school since Marilyn had left, and worst of all Justyn had been sent away to boarding school.

As Mother drove into the school drive to collect me that day, I opened the car door, and quavered, 'I am never ever going to school again.'

I never did. School phobia is also well recognised now, and backward or disturbed children are often withdrawn into small groups with special teachers. I know, because part of Tony's job is caring for these children, and I can tell him just what it feels like to be one of them! My parents had no support like that, but they were brave enough to do what needed to be done, and in the face of fierce criticism from family, friends and authorities, I stayed at home. A Danish lady called Marrianne came to be a nanny and governess rolled into one, and I loved her. Learning to read even at twelve can be great fun when no one is laughing at you. But the feeling of failure has never left me. Maybe that is why I am always striving to do something big and important just to prove myself.

Not going to school was wonderful at first, but then everything went terribly wrong. Father decided to move Hildenborough Hall to an Edwardian hotel on the sea front at Frinton. I missed the garden and the countryside quite desperately. There was nowhere to go for escape; even on the beach I felt spied on by hundreds of lace-curtained bathing huts. Marrianne hated it too, so she left and my home-based education was continued by a stream of retired school teachers. Frinton positively crawled with them. I was too terrified to go back to school, but I was also deeply ashamed and embarrassed because I didn't go.

Suddenly that day at Burrswood I looked back through the years and saw a revolting sight. Myself – a grossly overweight teenager stuffing herself with food behind the locked doors of her bedroom.

I ate because I was miserably lonely, but I dared not leave my room in case people would laugh at my hideous shape as well as my lack of ability. I was a total physical, mental and emotional mess, and I hated and despised myself.

'You were not alone in that room,' said Rosemary Anne gently, 'and even if you hated yourself Jesus was there loving you all the time. He understood how you felt. Let's picture Him there with you now, as we ask Him for His healing.'

As we did that, I suddenly realised how He *had* stepped into my life and rescued me.

'Everyone is good at something,' I remember 'the Boss' saying one day. 'Except me,' I had replied gloomily.

The modern theory of child-rearing is that parents must build their child's self-esteem by encouraging them in something they are good at doing. Mother and Father knew that without reading any books, and they must have worried about the state I was in, and prayed so much for wisdom. Father arranged music lessons and bought me a piano which he let me have in my bedroom. Considering his room was next to mine, and he spent many hours a day in it at that time, praying and studying the Bible, it was no small act of love on his part. He said he loved to hear my playing through the thin partition, and I actually believed him! He took a passionate interest in every new piece, and praised my discordant efforts. Because of his encouragement, in three years I was working for grade seven.

Mother played her part in my reclamation, by buying me a set of golf clubs and booking me a series of lessons with the local pro. At first I was almost too fat to see the ball, but soon I was a fully fledged member of the golf club, and when I was not playing the piano, I was endlessly hitting balls on the practice fairway. Suddenly I found I was the Essex Junior Champion, and poor Mother was hurtling me all over the country to national and international competitions. I had to keep fit to play well, so I lost weight, and travelling round to county matches and tournaments gave me self-confidence at last. What I hadn't realised before though, was how hard both my parents had to work to help the Lord answer their prayers!

Finally another miracle happened: even though I hadn't passed any exams, I got a place to train as a nanny. Though I still don't know how I had the cheek after the way I'd treated mine!

'Children of parents who are great achievers often feel guilty for just being normal,' commented Rosemary Anne.

83

'I don't think you'll dare to relax until you have lived up to your parents.'

So we prayed about that together and gave God the inferiority complex I had lived with ever since, and I know now that I am free of it.

But training as a nanny didn't prepare me for dealing with my second child, Justyn. After four years of hyperactive hell, I can remember standing in the middle of complete chaos, screaming hysterically.

I had spent all day preparing the house for special visitors, and gone upstairs to change just before the door bell was due to ring. When I came down, four-year-old Justyn had shaken scouring powder over the velvet suite, made flour castles on the carpet and squeezed toothpaste and washing-up liquid all over the carefully laid out tea. I knew from that moment how easy it could be for children to be battered. If it had not been for the grace of God, I would not have stopped short of murder!

Every theory of child-rearing Tony and I had learnt while training as teacher and nanny had been smashed. I could not take Justyn out because he had tantrums in supermarkets or bit other children we visited, and no one wanted to come to see me! As I stood there screaming, I really hated him, and felt he was spoiling my life.

I was in such helpless tears when the friends arrived that the wife took me upstairs to calm me down, while everyone else did the spring cleaning.

'I hate him, I think I have ever since he was born,' I sobbed. 'I thought mothers are supposed to love their children automatically. He's such an impossible child, do you think I should take him to a child guidance clinic?'

'I think Justyn's troubles stem from your relationship with him,' this very wise friend told me firmly. 'He doesn't need a psychiatrist, he just needs you to love him.'

'Love!' I exploded. 'But that's just what I can't seem to give him.'

'But love is not an automatic emotion,' she told me, 'it's an act of the will. Let God's love pour through you to him.' I must have looked a bit unconvinced. My knowledge of God had all retreated to my head by that stage in my life, leaving my heart very empty.

'Try a week of emergency prayer,' she encouraged.

'I haven't got time to pray for an hour, let alone a week!' I almost shouted.

'I realise that,' she said, 'but why not set the timer on your cooker to ring every half hour. When you hear it, stop whatever you are doing and lift Justyn up to God, and then re-set the timer for another half hour. God understands how exhausted you are.'

Even before the week was up, Justyn had changed completely, and even more important, I had relaxed and started to feel differently about him. It was not long afterwards that he was playing in the sandpit and suddenly asked if he could ask Jesus to come inside him.

He was certainly one of those troubled children I watched Jesus change. He is still hyperactive as a teenager, but all his energy goes into his many sports, hobbies and interests, and now I totally love him.

I wish I could say that incident brought me back to God again. It is so easy to turn to Him in a crisis and then drift away again when He answers our prayers and life improves. We still went to church, but our faith was all rather on the outside, until suddenly one morning I woke up and found I just did not believe anything any more.

It was a devastating feeling. Father had just died very suddenly, leaving my brother Justyn to take on the work of Hildenborough, and I suppose my relationship with God and my father were too closely bound. I just could not believe the world no longer contained him and now I had lost my faith, I could not believe Heaven existed to contain him either.

But God rescued me yet again; this time by a dream. On the night that should have been the Boss's birthday, I had gone to bed in a low state of misery. I was in mourning for

God as well as my father. Suddenly our bedroom door opened and in he walked, looking fit and well, and he sat down on the end of my bed as he always did in life.

'I've come with a very special message for you, Jen-Jen,' he said. 'Heaven *does* exist, and it's a lovely place. I want you to know that I am wonderfully happy there. But I also want you to realise that how you live on earth affects the way you enjoy it up here. Don't waste your life. Remember, "Only one life, 'twill soon be passed, only what's done for God will last!"' Then he was gone.

In the morning I desperately wanted to tell Tony about it but my throat felt as if I had swallowed a hard-boiled egg. I tried again to tell him as we were undressing for bed, but I was still too choked with grief. Tony is a very easy man to live with, and he never questions people about their private, deep feelings. He merely remarked as he got into bed, 'I've had such an odd day, you know how you can get a tune on the brain, and you keep singing it all the time until you're sick of it. Well, I haven't had a tune, but a kind of jingle, like a record over and over again. "Only one life, t'will soon be passed, only what's done for God will last." I can't remember hearing it before, have you?'

That finally broke me, and I told him the whole story. A few days later my brother was sorting through some papers, when he came upon a letter written by the Boss to Justyn and me some ten years before he died. I know this quote by heart.

'When you have finally got rid of me, don't ever forget this. There is "only one life, t'will soon be passed, only what's done for God will last". The world says eat, drink and be merry – we only have one life to enjoy, but a Christian knows that life is only a tiny, quickly passing fragment of his real existence, and pleasing God is the *only* thing worth doing with it.'

## Chapter Ten

When you are unmarried, you get into the habit of chatting to God as you dress, listening to Him talking through the Bible in a leisurely quiet time, and then falling asleep at night talking over the day's events with Him. But when you are married you talk things over with your husband instead. Soon you are dashing up in the morning to feed the baby, make breakfast for the children, sort the lunch boxes and find the PE kits.

I suddenly realised as I looked at Rosemary Anne what Paul meant in 1 Corinthians 7: 34: 'An unmarried woman concerns herself with the Lord's work because she wants to be dedicated both in body and spirit; but a married woman concerns herself with worldly matters, because she wants to please her husband.' From that moment I have always known that people who are called by God to be single are highly favoured by Him and very precious in His sight.

For although Tony and I had worked together in the Peacemakers and were equally dedicated to God, once we were married we didn't seem able to share Him. We tried to have our quiet times together each morning, but it just didn't work. We were so much in love we didn't want to go into different rooms, yet we felt inhibited praying with someone else in the room.

As baby followed baby in rapid succession, our times with God became shorter and shorter until they petered out completely. The church we attended was peacefully dying in its sleep, and spiritually so were we. It is terrifying how our

Christian lives can atrophy: as the practice goes, so does the desire. Nor can we live on past experiences; there is no such thing as 'spiritual capital' – it has to be a daily income.

Grinding on as a dutiful Christian was wearing me down, yet I couldn't help noticing that exciting things were happening to some of my friends whom I had known from Peacemaker or Hildenborough days. God was doing something new in people's lives – reviving them and giving them power and gifts I thought had gone out with the early church.

I was so intrigued that I spent nearly all the week's housekeeping money on books about this wave of blessing. But I got a nasty shock. Tony saw them lying on the kitchen table and he was furious.

'I'm not having books like that in the house,' he fumed, 'go out and burn them right now!'

Unfortunately for me, I had just read a book by Larry Christenson where he said that the wife's duty is to submit to her husband, thereby submitting through him to God. So off I trotted to the bonfire with *The Holy Spirit and You, They Speak in Other Tongues*, not to mention *Nine O'clock in the Morning*. As I watched the whole lot go up in flames, I couldn't help thinking sadly how many groceries their price would have bought!

Submission is easy enough on the odd occasion; but soon I was forgetting all about it, and beginning to feel that I should not let Tony 'hold me back'. He'd always been so easygoing that I had really become the dominant one – rather bossy really. I so desperately wanted a deeper relationship with God, that I mentally pushed him aside. I wanted this new excitement and power too much to wait any longer.

So I made a terrible mistake. Instead of praying earnestly about Tony's reaction, and then going to him and asking him if we could reconsider all these things together – which I'm sure he would have done – I never discussed it with him again, and it became a taboo area for us. It must already be obvious that Tony and I had a communication problem in our marriage. A shy person living with a very gregarious one must often have difficulties.

So, because I just would not wait, one day I put baby Naomi into her pram and pushed her off to a local park, and sitting by the lake I said, 'Lord if there is such a thing as Baptism in the Holy Spirit, and You think I need it, please do it for me now.'

Nothing seemed to happen, so rather drearily I went home to wash the nappies, but the next morning I felt completely different; a bit like someone who has always watched a black and white TV and then suddenly buys a colour set. I read the whole Bible through like a novel, suddenly it was a completely new book to me. At first when I tried to pray in tongues, I felt a complete idiot but as the embarrassment faded, I found this new form of prayer was refreshing to my whole being as it still is today. Sometimes I even found I knew just how to pray for people or what to say to them by supernatural knowledge, and once when I was visiting a little girl in my Bible class who was desperately ill with a painful and incurable disease, I felt compelled to place my hands on her and she began to get better.

But I kept it all a secret from Tony – I felt he would not approve of this new supernatural Christianity. I met masses of new charismatic friends in Tunbridge Wells where we were living then, and the gulf between Tony and me widened as I dashed from prayer meeting to praise group. We were no longer friends: I had excluded him from the most important area of my life. He was very absorbed in setting up a team teaching system in his school, and began to spend longer and longer in the company of other teachers and less and less time at home. They gave him the acceptance, companionship and friendship that I had effectively withdrawn.

I felt I had joined the ranks of the Christian elite. With all this wonderful new power, perhaps I could do the great work for God I had always longed to do. I felt it was my ministry to fill the house with crowds of people who needed help. So whenever Tony did come home he fell over women having nervous breakdowns or marriage problems. I became so absorbed in my rosy little spiritual life that Tony and my responsibilities as a wife disappeared behind the horizon.

Spiritual inferiority complexes are rife in Christian homes. Women at home with small children have so much more time to grow in the Lord through prayer and Bible study groups, while the men are out at work, that it can cause terrible tension. I thought Tony was unspiritual; he thought I didn't need him any more. We were drifting apart at a frightening pace and our marriage was disintegrating.

I realise now that God would never have allowed me to be 'held back'. I am convinced that if Satan cannot stop new waves of blessing, he tries to cause people to become spiritually proud because they have received new gifts, then he manages to bring divisions in churches, friendships and families. If only I had shared everything with Tony and let us move on together, we would have been saved so much unhappiness.

Finally, God rescued us by allowing sorrow and stress to come our way. As Samuel Rutherford wrote, 'God hath more ways of hunting for our love than one or two.' We had not planned a fourth baby – I didn't want to disrupt what I saw as my 'ministry'. (I have come to loathe that word used in its present-day form. It sounds so arrogant; Jesus sends us to serve, to be slaves for the gospel and not superstars!) But Naomi had been such an easy child after the horrors of Justyn, that I wasn't too worried when I found I was pregnant again. In fact, I thought I was a pretty good mother by then; God certainly has used Duncan to topple my pride!

I knew there was something badly wrong with him by the time he was five days old, for he was in constant pain. He was born with a rare disease of the digestive system, and everything shot through the poor little chap, virtually unprocessed. He hung on to life somehow for several weeks, and then the consultant said, 'I am very sorry, but there is no more we can do.' It is a terrible feeling looking down into a hospital cot and realising your baby is dying, and no human can do anything about it.

Tony and I sat in the little cubicle with Duncan, and I remember gripping the radiator, feeling I wanted to shake it off the wall.

'I was reading the Beatitudes this morning,' said Tony, and his voice was coming from hundreds of miles away. 'Happy are they that mourn for God will comfort them.'

'I don't want to be comforted,' I stormed, 'I just want my baby to live.'

That evening Trevor Deering was preaching in Tunbridge Wells at a healing service. 'I'm going to that,' I said, 'you stay here with Duncan.' It was a huge meeting, packed to the doors, and at the end I went up and asked Trevor Deering to pray for Duncan. But when I got back to the hospital Duncan looked just as white and lifeless as he had when I left him.

But the next day something happened. The consultant came round again, and told us they were going to have one last try, feeding him with a new substance. 'So long as he eats nothing else whatever, it may just keep him ticking over until he gets stronger.' Valactin did that. It kept him alive – just – and for fifteen months we fed it to him through a bottle every three hours, day and night.

They were ghastly months. He developed breathing problems as well, so I had to do all my housework with him strapped in a carry seat on my back. Being upright helped him to breathe, and the warmth of my body soothed his tummy pain.

It was confusing. Why did God not fully heal him? I had laid hands on him in faith so many times, many people were praying and several with healing ministries visited us, but still I had to care for a little shrivelled wheezing monkey, hanging on to life by a thread. Why?

It could not be God's fault, so it must be mine. One evening after a desperate day when I really had had enough of his wails and wheezes, there at the door was our vicar, Donald Eddison – one of the most gentle people I have ever known. The look of sympathy in his eyes broke me down finally.

'He'd get better if I only had more faith,' I wept.

'No, no,' replied Donald gently. 'Never have faith *in* faith, it's only *His* faithfulness that counts.' Suddenly all the guilt and blame slid from me, and I was smiling as I showed him out of the front door later.

'Wait for God's time,' he said, as he stood on the doormat. 'It's always perfect.'

Because we had to wait fifteen months for His Perfect Time, Tony and I were drawn right back close together again, as we literally struggled for survival through the sleepless nights and exhausting days. We had time together at last because I could not be out at praise meetings, and the only people I had time to 'minister' to were my own four far from easy children.

Of course God didn't *cause* Duncan to be ill, but I think He does use the natural difficulties of life to bless us – and we really were greatly blessed by Duncan's illness.

Some time before Duncan was born I had managed to persuade Tony to come to a large charismatic gathering with me – I can't think how! We were met at the door by a well-meaning but massively tactless friend who beamed at Tony, and said, 'I didn't realise you had been "filled".' Tony was filled all right, but unfortunately it was with rage and not with the Spirit, and he vowed never to go near anything like that again.

So when Juan Carlos Ortis came to Tunbridge Wells I did not for one minute expect Tony to come with me. But it had been so many long months since we had been out together, that we trusted Duncan to Gom, just for once, and decided to go. We were both deeply blessed that night, and when Juan Carlos asked anyone who wanted to rededicate their lives completely to God's service to take off their coats and tie them around their waists as a sign that they would serve God in any and every way He desired, Tony's jacket came off before anyone else had their buttons undone.

Tony does not talk much, everything happens inside him, but two days later he said suddenly. 'The difference between consecrating one's life to God and receiving the Baptism of the Holy Spirit, is that when you *give* you can be proud that you were willing to give that much, but when you *receive* you can only feel humbled at receiving such an enormous amount.' That is all he ever said, but we were together again walking side by side, and right from that time we have actually enjoyed praying together daily.

It is a strange thing, but the week we moved into the peace of the country in Mayfield, Duncan was due to go back into hospital for a biopsy and other horrid tests (they thought he had cystic fibrosis among other things). He was just beginning to crawl, and while I was preoccupied with the hassle of moving in, he got into the larder and went through a box of groceries which lay on the floor. When I realised what he had eaten I was horrified. Even a tiny spoonful of the different foods the hospital had tested him with periodically had caused a violent reaction. Now he had gorged biscuits, sugar lumps, a cheese triangle, silver paper and all, and taken several bites out of an onion. When you have never actually eaten anything in your life, that is quite a lot!

'Good,' said the hospital when I rang them, 'as soon as he gets the reaction, bring him right over and we'll do the biopsy at once.' We are still waiting for that reaction, the next wheeze and the biopsy! God healed Duncan in his own perfect time and saved our marriage from foundering.

## Chapter Eleven

It was most humiliating for me to feel the same furious rage at the beginning of the last session with Rosemary Anne, as I had felt on the first, and this time I was not three, but well into my thirties. My only slight comfort was that I was pounding the walls of our lounge and hurting my fists instead of scratching to ribbons the person with whom I was really angry.

'Lord,' I heard myself pray, 'why don't You just take her to Heaven right now. She'll never be happy again down here, and she's driving me mad!'

It seemed terrible to pray that your mother would die, but I knew how she longed for Heaven.

When Father died she did not just lose a husband, she lost her work and her home. They had been together for so long, praying, working and uniting their gifts, that the shock of his death finally disintegrated her health. It was only right that she should leave Hildenborough to give Justyn and his wife Joy complete freedom to run the place in their own way, but when you have lived in a community for so long and are totally undomesticated, as well as having a rapidly deteriorating heart condition, you cannot really manage on your own.

She did not completely live with us, but we combined with Father's mother Lolo, and bought a house in the country big enough for us all to have a kitchen. It worked wonderfully well with Lolo, who was fit and well at nearly ninety, but with Mother it was a disaster. Her body may have worn out, but her mind still raced on, and she had no one now to organise but us! She rattled through a series of housekeeper-companions, becoming more and more depressed as her frustration grew.

Finally we just had to admit failure, and when we lost Lolo, we decided to split up and Mother began a life of private hotels and nursing homes in Tunbridge Wells. As her health became worse, senile dementia began to grip her mind and she was just not the same loving, outgoing person who had helped many thousands of people. In fact, her illness made her so impossible that she quarrelled continually with each nursing home and hotel, and Justyn, Tony and I constantly had the embarrassing job of moving her and her possessions on to the next place, until we almost exhausted even the vast list in Tunbridge Wells.

It was unbearable to see her like that, and Tony and I were constantly asking ourselves, 'What shall we do about Otty?' (as we all called her).

Of course we felt we should have her to live with us again, but my relationship with her had never been a very easy one. Her beauty, gifts and personality had always accentuated my own sense of inadequacy and I felt she despised me for just being a housewife and mother. Somehow, beside her I felt like a lumbering cart-horse next to a beribboned Derby winner.

'But when she had deteriorated physically and mentally, why did you still feel like that?' probed Rosemary Anne.

'Well,' I confessed, 'that irritated me just as much. With numerous small children of my own and fostering other people's, I had to live at a high speed, and her slowness infuriated me. And I never could cope with illness and handicap anyway.' Even as I said that, a cold feeling spread over me – if I could not cope with that in other people, how was I going to cope with it myself, and would my family feel as irritated by my incapacities as I had been by my mother's?

Vividly I remember the awful burden of guilt. We had her over one day a week, and I rang every day, but I still lived with the feeling that I was neglecting her. I knew she longed to come and live with us again and felt lonely and rejected, but I also knew I just could not cope.

When she had her stroke the whole thing came to a head. We realised it meant a geriatric ward or a full-scale nursing home after that, but I had visited such places, and heard the confused old people endlessly calling for the people they loved, and praying just to die.

That is why I started pounding our walls. Why could she not just die? I could not live with myself if I abandoned her to strangers, but she was only sixty-six and might live for years, and if she came to us what would happen to the 'work' I was going to do for God once the children were off my hands?

'What are you trying to do to me, Lord!' I raged, as I pounded the walls. 'Richard is only two, Jane needs so much time, and with the other four as well, how can you want me to look after a senile, incontinent invalid? Just take her home to Heaven, and solve everyone's problems.'

But He didn't. I'm glad now: He had so much to teach us. We were in our little church in Mayfield the following Sunday, and Sarah, who was then about twelve, suddenly passed her Bible along the pew, pointing vigorously to some verses in 1 Timothy 5. Hurriedly I read them, and felt my cheeks turning scarlet. 'But if a widow has children or grandchildren they should learn first to carry out their religious duties towards their own family and in this way repay their parents and grandparents because that is what pleases God. But if anyone does not take care of his relatives, especially the members of his own family, he has denied the faith and is worse than an unbeliever' (1 Tim. 5: 4, 8).

'Look at that, Mum!' said Sarah, in a hoarse whisper everyone in church could hear. 'We *ought* to have Otty to live with us.'

We went home and held a family council round the Sunday lunch table. All the childen agreed with Sarah, Tony was his usual easy self, only I knew I just could not cope.

'We'll pray about it,' I said weakly, but that afternoon as I did so, I saw a picture of myself hurtling at speed towards a brick wall on which I felt sure I would smash myself. But I knew the Lord wanted us to have her, and the children confirmed that conviction.

I don't think that *all* Christian families should care for their elderly relatives at home. The Lord must guide individually in each case. He knew I would not find it easy to cope, but He also knew I would not *have* to for long, so He gave me just enough strength and patience for the seven months more that she lived.

When she had her second stroke I was just about reaching cracking point, and the doctor said, 'Hospital I think,' when he looked at me. But I knew her one great fear was to die alone, so we decided to get private nurses to come in for a few hours each day, to give me a break.

'We're going to the sea, for some fresh air,' Tony said that Sunday, when the nurse arrived. It was so lovely after having been shut in the house for so many months. On the way home I was sitting in the back to keep the boys from fighting, and I suddenly realised I could not face arriving home. I just could not keep my mother any longer, my energy had run out. What shall I do, Lord?' I remember whispering, and then I saw that brick wall again, and I was still rushing towards it. The impact was imminent, and I braced myself for it, but as I reached that wall it just dissolved.

'I'll never test you above what you are able,' I heard the Lord say.

When we reached home, the nurse told us that Mother's condition had deteriorated suddenly. A few hours later she died, just as she would have liked to have done, with her son holding one hand, and me the other.

Looking after her like that to the end didn't exactly heal the guilt, though I am sure that's mostly why I did it. But guilt can't be dealt with by just doing positive things, and not letting God free us of the past. When she died the guilt about my feeling for her really set in hard.

One night I had a terrible nightmare. I was washing her in bed, as I had every day for all those months, but suddenly she was a skeleton. Only her eyes were alive, reproaching me for the way I was really feeling about her inside. I knew I needed help so I went straight round to my friend Rhoda, who had often prayed with me about things that troubled us both. Together we confessed my guilt to the Lord, and she asked Him for definite healing.

As she stood beside me, her hands on my shoulders, I saw that reproachful skeleton again, but as I watched, it fell away from me into a dark valley and I looked up to what seemed like a sunlit mountain top. There I saw Mother standing happily next to the Boss. She was wearing one of the feathery hats she always loved, and they both waved, reassuring me once again of their continued and happy existence in Heaven.

I did feel healed after that, though it never seemed quite fair to me that someone who had served God so faithfully should have been allowed ten such terrible years at the end.

That night, when Rosemary Anne had gone, I picked up Mother's worn old Bible from beside my bed. It had been such a joy to me at Burrswood. I could not read long passages, but I was fascinated by her heavy underlining of certain verses, which must have been very important to her. That night the tiny phrase 'But if not' caught my eye. It could hardly have failed to do so, seeing it was circled in red: Daniel 3: 18 (AV).

Suddenly I saw us at breakfast long ago, Justyn in his high chair, Nanny fussing round him, and me with egg on my face, while Mother told us the story of Shadrach, Meshach and Abednego so vividly that we could see the billowing flames, and feel the heat from that fiery furnace.

'What god is able to deliver you from me?' mocked the wicked king, while my egg grew cold.

'Our God is able to deliver us . . . but if not . . .' (Dan. 3: 17–18 AV) and I remember Mother actually crying with emotion as she told us that even though they knew God could deliver them from the flames, they were still prepared to trust Him even if He did not. In the margin and also in red Mother had added, 'Job said "If He slay me yet will I trust Him."' A little further on in her Bible I found this poem which must have dated from those last ten sad years.

> I thank you Lord for trusting me with pain
> That I should suffer loss, and so should gain
> Gold of experience tempered in God's fire,
> O Lord through suffering only we acquire
> Those priceless riches of Eternity,
> That soul enlargement, fellowship with thee.

I fell asleep with the happy knowledge that even if I did not understand why God had allowed her suffering and however muddled and agitated her mind had become, she had never lost her total love for the Lord. As soon as she stepped into Heaven, He would have explained to her *all* His reasons for allowing it! (2 Cor. 4: 16–17).

'I've found a verse for you,' I said when I saw Rosemary Anne next day – my last at Burrswood. 'Proverbs 20: 5: "A person's thoughts are like water in a deep well, but someone with insight can draw them out."'

She had done that so gently and so perceptively, and taught me what a wonderful form of healing this can be. I felt clean right through my whole being, and – yes – excited. I had looked back over forty years and realised He had been there to heal me in every crisis of my life, so He was not going to fail me now.

I left Burrswood full of hope, feeling healed spiritually, mentally and physically. I was growing stronger each day, and suddenly it was good to be alive again.

We did not go home straight away, but spent two weeks at Hildenborough Hall, where Tony was organising the children's activities at the family weeks Max was running. I stayed quietly in my room all the time on doctor's orders, but it was a wonderful opportunity to remake the relationships with Tony and the children without actually having to care for them. They were all rather shy of me at first, but when one evening Richard climbed into bed beside me and said, 'Tell me a story,' I knew I was accepted again.

While we were there we had our wedding anniversary, and Tony took the day off and we went out together, just the two of us. It was one of those golden days that never fade in your mind. There was so much to talk about, and time to get it all said without the end of visiting hour waiting to cut us off.

There was something we badly needed to discuss. The doctor at Burrswood had called Tony aside before we left and said, rather ominously, 'Your wife will have to have completely full-time living-in help for at least eighteen months – no household responsibilities whatever, and she must spend most of every day resting.'

'We can't do that!' I protested in horror when Tony brought up the subject as we drove along the Kentish lanes. 'Our budget wouldn't even run to an hour's cleaning a week, let alone a full-time nanny/housekeeper/nurse/chauffeur – even if we could ever find such a paragon of virtue. And anyway,' I almost sobbed, 'I couldn't possibly have some strange woman running my house, I wouldn't have a reason for living any more.'

Cooking, washing and cleaning have always been my ways of showing love to my family and if I may have been 'just a housewife' at least that did give me some status in the world. '*And*,' I finished firmly, 'I'm being healed, and coping by myself will be good for my floppy muscles. You must *fight* illness, not sit about and rest all day!'

Tony understood, bless him, and said with a wry smile, 'I can always give you a hand, I'm pretty good with fish fingers now.'

We wanted to go into the little church in Otford where we had been married, at just that exact time sixteen years before, and as we knelt side by side at the rail we thanked God together that Tony had not had to face this day alone. We also thanked Him for preserving our marriage through

100

some rough patches, and bringing us so close together, but there was something more we wanted to do. Certainly we wanted to thank the Lord for His steady daily healing, but we also felt we should ask for a definite leap forward, a speeding up, a big dollop of health as an anniversary present.

As we rose from our knees, I handed Tony my stick, 'I won't be needing that now,' I beamed, 'and I'll flush all my pills down the loo and leave the Lord to control my heart beat and do all the other things they're supposed to do. From now on I am *living in my healing!*'

When we reached the car we paused and looked at each other. 'I just know I am completely healed, so why shouldn't I drive up to Hildenborough?' I said.

Tony gulped, as faith and common sense fought each other, but faith won, and he handed me the car keys. He is always tense being driven by anyone, so that journey must have been terrifying for him, but five minutes later we landed safely, and as I pulled on the handbrake a wonderful thought struck me.

'Now I'm healed, we won't have to leave our lovely home and garden – we can stay in the country and live happily ever after!'

'We promised the Lord and the estate agent we would leave it till September,' replied Tony doggedly. 'We must keep our word.'

But our house had once suffered badly from subsidence, and everyone who viewed it threw up their hands in horror when they saw the cracks in the walls. By September no one had shown any interest in buying it. I could not help feeling a bit like Abraham when he found the ram in the thicket, and did not have to offer up his beloved son Isaac.

God had given me back my home – I had asked Him for a continuous joyous relationship with Him, but He had also healed me!

*Chapter Twelve*

I was positively bubbling with excitement as we left Hildenborough. 'Lord make me an instrument of thy peace at home,' I wrote in my black book that morning, but several weeks later, I notice, I added a bitter little comment beside the entry: 'Ha blooming Ha!'

Selwyn Hughes says it is only too easy for Christians to confuse faith with presumption and it only took a few hours of being home for me to realise I was a cripple in body and mind. In hospital, at Burrswood and even in my room at Hildenborough, I had been sheltered from the real world of healthy people. Now they swarmed round me like ants in a disturbed ant heap.

I shall never forget Richard's first morning at school. I was determined to go with Tony and take him, even though I had not been out 'in public' before. As we reached the school gates I felt pierced by the stares of other children and their mums. They gazed at my suddenly emaciated body as it twitched and shook and reeled across the playground like a drunkard's. Some looked at me with pity in their eyes, which I hated, while others I had known for years turned away and pretended I was just not there.

Cooking was a nightmare. I hardly had the muscular strength to put a dish in the oven, and no feelings in my hands to tell me it was dangerously hot when I took it out. The vacuum cleaner became a monster with a will of its own, and without my stick I fell frequently because I could neither balance nor feel my feet. The family's recurring gag became

'What did you break today, Mum?' as my fingers, which would not grip, daily sent our china crashing to destruction. But it was my speech which caused them the most hilarity. I became increasingly unable to express what I wanted to say, and no one will ever forget the day I told Duncan to eat his clothes before putting on his cornflakes! My mind felt like a house gutted by fire – a burnt-out wreck. My ability to think was gone, and I could not even remember how long fish fingers take to cook.

The utter frustration and weakness made me terribly bad-tempered. I felt the children had run as wild as the garden in my absence, and soon I was constantly nagging about tidiness and table manners, and foolishly over-reacting to muddy footmarks and unbrushed hair. They must have wished I had never come home.

'You can't go on like this!' said my friend Penny (Brian's wife) when she discovered me one day, trying to do the ironing in a cold sweat of weakness. 'We'll organise a rota of church members – we'll take everything over from you. It will be a wonderful way to demonstrate to the whole village the ministry of caring.' But in my pride I did not want to be on the receiving end of anyone's 'ministry'.

'No thanks,' I said firmly, 'I couldn't bear the house full of people all the time, I just want to be left alone to get on with it.'

She was hurt, and I did not deserve friends like that. But I just wanted to run away from people because I was not the glowing Christian witness I felt I ought to be – I was too tired. Nor could I stand people seeing how mutilated I was. I was brain-damaged, and I could not even speak clearly enough to hold a conversation. So I locked the doors to prevent people popping in as they always do in the country, and if I heard someone ring the bell, I hid. They soon got the message, and stopped coming. How I thank God that Grace had already learnt how to break into our house. She continued to do so every morning, insisting on taking the children to school, and having a quick time of prayer with me before they left. She has suffered many things in her life, and I felt she accepted me as I was, and never made comments or offered sympathy and advice. We have prayed together regularly ever since.

One evening Tony found me standing at the window gazing helplessly over the garden. The apples needed picking, the vegetables were ready to go down in the freezer, and everywhere needed an autumn tidy-up, but I did not even have the energy to open a tin of baked beans.

'That's why I wanted to move, darling,' he said gently. 'Starting a new life would have been easier than not being able to live the old one.'

'But I *will* get better!' I stormed repeatedly, as the chaos mounted around us. I had once been so proud of my spotless house – how ridiculous that seemed now.

Two of my mother's sisters were so concerned in the end that they paid for us to have someone in to clean several times a week, or I really think the children might have become ill from living in unsanitary conditions.

I did not mind Melody coming in because she was paid to do so, but I was not going to sponge on other Christians. I seemed to have forgotten all the joy I had received from cleaning other people's houses, and cooking them meals in my old 'Martha' days. All I managed to do was to make myself bitterly lonely, and hurt a lot of people as well as robbing them of the blessing God would have given them for helping us. It *is* much more blessed to give than to receive, and also much more pleasant for the ego!

The inevitable consequence of my pride was a relapse. The doctors had warned me that if I did not rest the inflammation would begin to increase again. Soon the pain in my spine and head was quite indescribable. The high-voltage painkillers did not help the vertigo, and I was soon too nauseated to eat. The slightest thing sent me into a panic, but still my pride would not let me admit defeat and rest was still a rude word.

Quite the most devastating thing of all was that I seemed to have lost the closeness of my relationship with the Lord.

For years I had looked forward to Richard going to school so I could have time on *my own* to study the Bible and pray. Now he was out all day, I missed him desperately and felt redundant and lonely, while prayers seemed never to penetrate the ceiling and the Bible felt just a boring jumble of meaningless words.

'You are not playing fair, Lord,' I burst out one morning as I struggled to scrub the egg from the breakfast plates. 'I asked You that night in hospital for a *continuous* close relationship, but I couldn't feel further away from You if I was Judas! I thought You'd healed me, but in fact I am getting worse!'

But He did not answer me, and so I muddled on with the help of quantities of painkillers until, quite suddenly, I went into the dark valley. Of course, I had forgotten about the vision He had given me in London, warning me of the depression to come, so I was completely devastated.

By then I was just beginning to be able to concede that it might be possible for God to allow a Christian to succumb to a physical illness for several good reasons, but it was quite impossible for a Christian to be depressed. That, in all the books I had read, was caused by inner conflict or buried sin, and I had just spent a whole long exhausting week having my memories healed. If I had gone to the doctor he would have told me depression hits most people after such a serious illness. But I wouldn't go – I thought he might label me as a mental case. I did not mention it to Tony, Grace or anyone else, I was too deeply ashamed, but a terrible black cloud descended over my head, tangible and suffocating.

No pain or illness is as bad as depression, and you cannot believe it will ever end. In all other forms of illness, distress, bereavement or suffering of any kind a Christian can feel conscious of God's presence, but one of the symptoms of depression is the loss of joy in the Lord, the assurance of His love, and often the belief in His existence.

I have to confess that I had always been slightly irritated by depressed people, feeling sure that their problems were brought on by their own self-centred attitude – all they needed to do was to stop thinking about themselves and start praising the Lord. I sense that quite a few Christian people think like this – until depression hits them as well! Proverbs 25 verse 20 says, 'Singing to a depressed person is like taking off his clothes on a cold day, or rubbing salt into a wound.' I quickly learnt the truth of that verse, and could not go near church or even Burrswood for months. After all, God had not healed me, so He could not really love me.

The black cloud was always worse first thing in the morning, and if I had managed to sleep at all it hit me as I woke, feeling more like a ton of wet sand than a cloud. However could I face another day?

I would have been far worse off without the children. Because of them I *had* to get up and see them off to school complete with lunch boxes, and although the lethargy of depression made me want to lie in bed all day with a pillow over my face, I had to cook a meal for them all in the evening, and that often took me three or four hours at least!

Of course I had deliberately cut myself off from people, but another symptom of depression is feeling no one cares about you any more, and I was bitterly lonely, after always living in a house full of people. Now the phone and the door bell never rang, and each day seemed like a week.

Somehow I could not bring myself to address the Almighty direct, but communicated with Him through my diary. I am embarrassed to read it now, and only comforted by the fact that Job, when he was ill and depressed, expressed his feelings to God in much the same rude fashion. I must have gone on reading my Bible each day and heavily underlined and positively wallowed in such passages as Psalms 42, 69, and 102, not to mention Lamentations Chapter 3.

I am one who knows what it is to be punished by God. He drove me deeper and deeper into darkness and beat me again and again with merciless blows. He has left my flesh open and raw and has broken my bones. He has shut me in a prison of misery and anguish . . . He rubbed my face in the ground and broke my teeth on the gravel. I have forgotten what health and peace and happiness are . . . my hope in the Lord is gone.

(Lam. 3: 1–5, 16–18)

Only a few months before, the Lord had been everything I wanted my life to contain. His love had been a constant hourly joy; now He was a brutal punishing tyrant. What had I done to lose His company and comfort? I missed Him unutterably.

One entry in my prayer diary says, 'Lord, these pages are full of requests, which You never seem to answer, how come?' A few days later: 'All right Lord, so You don't care about me any more, but You might at least help me to be less bad-tempered with the children! All this must be hell for Tony.'

However horrible depression is, I think it must be harder to live with depression than to *be* depressed. Tony just thought I was in severe physical pain, but I could see his spirits drooping, just when he was becoming happy again after my experience with Father Keith. I exhausted myself by making frantic efforts to lift the gloom I knew I was creating, only to be cut to the heart one day at tea time, when Sarah remarked, 'We never seem to laugh any more these days.' How responsible a mother is for the atmosphere of a family!

Looking back on it all now, I can see how good God was to give me that vision in London of the dark valley, and gently to explain to me His reasons for allowing me to go through it. That helps me now to understand that depression, but strangely it did not help me at the time. Never once during those dark months did I look backwards in my diary and recall that vision. I suppose if I had I would never have learnt one of the main lessons He wanted me to learn through that experience. When we belong to Him, He *is* with us whether we feel it or even believe it. All through that dark valley His 'everlasting arms' were beneath me (Deut. 33: 27 AV), even when I did not *realise* it. His presence with us does not depend on our feelings or our faith, it just happens to be a fact!

I can see from my diary how serious things were becoming when I read entries like, 'I am lost. Life is quite hopeless. Why didn't I just die on June 2nd when I had the chance? Tony and the children would all be happier without me. I am just a useless zombie. Perhaps I should destroy myself before I damage my family any more.' What would the village say? I thought cynically as I lay in the bath one night. I have spent years gossiping about how wonderful God is, they'll hardly believe me when I'm found hanging.

It was only a kind of game at first – planning my suicide, but one day I discovered an old bottle of my mother's sleeping pills and stood in the middle of my bedroom holding them in my hand for a dangerously long time. I could take them all, and then stagger into the wood, so the children did not find me when they came home. How easy it would be. With a shudder of horror I threw them back into the drawer, but the idea stayed with me night and day. Suddenly I realised that I needed help urgently. It was my pride I needed to swallow, not a bottle of Mogadon.

I had to go to the Kent and Sussex for one of my boring out-patient checks, so very nervously I made an appointment to see George on the same day. I was literally shaking with fright as I knocked on the door marked Hospital Chaplain.

'I'm terribly sorry,' I apologised, 'but I seem to have gone into a depression.' To my relief he did not seem to be shocked or even surprised. He did not need all the gory details, nor did he probe into the reasons or try to detect the 'root sin'.

'You must not feel guilty about this depression,' he said gently. 'You are feeling absolutely ghastly, and when Jesus felt like that on the cross He told His Father just how He felt, and cried out to Him in the darkness. So He understands *just* how you are feeling now. We are going to do just what He did, but we're also going to ask the Father to take this depression away.'

There was no oil, or laying on of hands – no 'going down under the Spirit' – he just asked God to take it away and God did, and suddenly I felt that cloud lift off the top of my head.

I really cannot say I 'went on my way rejoicing' because when you have been depressed for a long time your mind gets into the habit of it, and has to be reprogrammed. But the next morning I woke waiting for the now familiar weight to drop, and it did not. That night I recorded in my diary, 'Felt groggy physically all day but not *one bit depressed*!'

Being George, he had not let me off scot free! 'Take one verse from the Bible each day,' he told me, 'and repeat it over and over as you work round the house, but each time emphasise a different word:

> *My* grace is sufficient for you
> My *grace* is sufficient for you
> My grace is *sufficient* for you
> My grace is sufficient for *you*.'

It is just as well that our house was right out in the wilds, because if any of the village gossips had looked at me through my window and seen me muttering, 'I *can* do all things through Christ,' while watering the house plants, and setting the table while shouting, 'My strength is made perfect in weakness,' the village grapevine would have had me certified!

But at the beginning there was one verse I just could not manage – 'The joy of the Lord is my strength' – because I had to re-learn what joy was.

It is extraordinary how healthy and happy everyone else looks when you are feeling depressed. Even television adverts are irritating! When a friend gave us tickets for the opera *Fidelio* in Eastbourne, I felt deeply threatened by all the laughing faces around me, and did not enjoy my evening out until the house lights went down and the curtains rose.

During the wonderful scene when the prisoners are led out of their dark dungeon into the light of freedom, I whispered, 'Lord, I've been in captivity like them, I know I'm coming out into the light now, but I've lost all my joy.'

'Have mine then,' He replied through the glorious crescendo of music.

It's all very well saying 'have mine', I thought as we drove home through the fog and rain, but practically speaking, how can I get it?

As usual, I knew the answer in theory. *It is the act of praise that brings the joy, not the joy that brings the praise.* That night I looked up two of my favourite 'depressed' passages, and was suddenly struck by the antidote to depression the Bible so clearly gives. Psalm 69 was so full of gloom that I had loved it, but the sudden change comes between verses 29 and 30. 'I am in pain and despair, lift me up O God, and save me!' How often I had pleaded with Him, seemingly in vain to save me, but verse 30 gives the answer: 'I will praise God with a song, I *will* proclaim his greatness by giving him thanks.' Then I looked up Lamentations 3: 19–24: 'The thought of my pain . . . is bitter poison, I think of it constantly and my spirit is depressed, *yet hope returns to me* when I remember this one thing: the Lord's unfailing love and mercy still continue . . . the Lord is all I have, and so I put my hope in him.'

Somehow it had to be an act of will on my part to praise Him when nothing seemed to be going right, and trust Him when everything else seemed to have vanished. I found many other passages in the Bible with this theme, but I still firmly believe that this cure for depression cannot be forced on to a depressed person. Had George told me, when I went to see him in depression, 'The Bible says just praise the Lord and everything will be fine,' I might well have hit him! What comforted me then was to know that Jesus really did know how terrible I felt, and through George's prayer for me the Lord Himself opened my eyes to the Bible's way out of depression.

'But I don't know how to praise you, Lord,' I gulped as I

weakly looked round the bomb site which is my house after the children have left for school. Even with Melody's help with cleaning there was still a terrifying amount of tiny little jobs that made up my day. I would stand and sweat with panic as I faced the mountain of clean washing which had to be sorted into eight different piles, and lunch boxes were a nightmare, trying to remember seven various likes and dislikes.

I started to force myself to see each little job as something actually done for God. I implored His help at the beginning, imagined Him watching me as I did it as an offering for Him, and finally thanked Him with relief when it was finished, and before I started to panic about the next job. I did not feel like praising Him, and I often had to do it through clenched teeth. But at last one day I remember cleaning some mud-encrusted hockey boots, and shouting, 'The joy of the Lord *is* my strength!'

Slowly it began to take effect – I can actually see the entries in my prayer diary changing in nature. At first they were screams for help and deliverance, then endless little personal requests like, 'Lord, show me what to wear today,' and 'What shall I cook for tea?' People in depression are totally turned in on themselves. They cannot help it; it is a symptom of the illness, like spots with measles, but after a while I found myself praying for Tony and the children. Then as I forced myself to make contact again with other people, I began to be concerned for their needs and prayed about their problems, a sure sign I was on the mend. Finally one morning I wrote, 'Lord I seem to come to You each morning with a list of things *I want You to do for me or others*. Please help me to ask You first what You want *me* to do for *You*.'

Through that depression – ghastly as it was – I learnt a new reliance on the Lord. If I had never reached the point of utterly devastating inability, I might never have realised how much I need His help in the little things as well as in the big things of life. I had asked Him that night in the Kent and Sussex Hospital for a continuous relationship of worship.

Dimly I began to see that He could be worshipped through the ordinary little jobs of every day just as easily as He can be in church on Sundays.

When that landmark of the fortieth birthday arrived, and it dawned on me that I probably never would achieve any great world-shaking work for God, it was a deep comfort to realise that the two words for worship and serve are the same in Hebrew. Just as I could worship Him while I washed the dishes and made the sandwiches, I was also serving Him when each tiny act was done for Him. I do, however, have to admit that it would be much happier for the ego if one was called to do something for the Lord that other people noticed as well!

## Chapter Thirteen

'How are you?' beamed a Christian friend one day as I struggled round the village supermarket.

'Fine!' I lied as I contorted my face into what I hoped was a 'good Christian smile'. Actually I felt ghastly, but other Christians expect you to be problem free and constantly victorious, and I felt I had to live up to their expectations or I would let the Lord down.

'You're coping all right then?' she continued, in the tone of voice that demands only the answer yes.

'Melody does the things I can't manage,' I told her.

'How wonderful,' gushed my friend. 'She will see such a grand Christian witness in your home.' I gulped and my smile slipped a bit. Right between the shelves of baked beans and biscuits it dawned on me that I was living a double life; putting on my Christian smile like a hat when I went out. At home Melody did not see a patient Christian nobly putting up with trials, but a bear with a sore head – the grizzly kind!

As I crawled home, I felt the size and shape of a slug. Suddenly my mind went back to the days of the Peace-makers, and I remembered one of the group called George. He had many problems in his life. 'Christians should always be happy and cheerful whatever they go through,' he was told. 'Then I can't really be a Christian after all,' he said hopelessly, and hanged himself in despair.

George was more honest than I am, I thought, as I felt once again the shock of his death.

I have observed Christian friends going through terrible

crises and bereavements, and their radiant witness to the world builds your faith in the reality and loving kindness of the Lord. But when the acute stage is over or if their problems are long term, a very human reaction can set in – just when their Christian friends feel they should be 'getting over it'.

This is just what happened to Job. At first he coped with his trials in triumph, saying, 'The Lord gave, and the Lord has taken away, blessed be the name of the Lord' (Job 1: 21 RSV). But when his illness had dragged wearily on for months – if not years – he started behaving very badly saying the most outrageous things. Yet God still loved him, and it was in those dark times that Job said, 'Though He slay me, yet will I trust Him.'

At least Job was honest with his friends, even if he did shock them. But in these days of stereotypes we feel Christians should be perpetually joyful, and if we don't feel like that, we force ourselves to pretend. But aren't we forgetting that we are human beings? We must allow ourselves and one another to hurt sometimes, and we have to keep remembering that we all react to things differently. What may be an enormous trauma to one person is only a slight annoyance to another. God sees us as individuals – when will we learn to do the same!

'I'm a hypocrite!' I confessed to a friend later that day. 'But everyone I meet says, "How are you?" so what *am* I supposed to say?'

Betty grinned at me over her coffee cup. 'Just say, "I've got lots to thank the Lord for." It's always true, however ghastly life may be, and it also honours God.'

Of course it is wrong for us to grovel around constantly moaning about our problems; the more we talk about them the bigger they seem. But I have become convinced that we need to be more honest with each other. Someone came to see me the other day who has recently lost her husband, her home and almost everything else she valued.

'I am baffled and hurting,' she told me. 'But I know the

114

Lord will help me through.' I felt she was so much more genuine than I was when I went about wearing a fixed smile and saying 'I'm fine, I haven't any problems.'

The wonderful thing is that although I felt so embarrassed about my bad witness to Melody, she still found the Lord, though in spite of me and not because of me. When she answered my advertisement in the sweet-shop window, she was already searching for God because her sister had recently found Him, and had started to pray for her. She began asking me questions about God as she scrubbed the floors or cleaned the windows.

'You Christians always seem so happy,' she said one day, and I nearly died of surprise. Perhaps joy is something we have whether we actually feel it or show it. We don't have to put it on – it is there underlying everything when Jesus lives in us. Happiness depends on happenings, but He promised us His joy no matter what we have to go through.

Melody became such a good friend, it seemed like the end of the world when she said she had to leave because she was moving house. But as always the Lord helped us, though He certainly sent the help in an extraordinary package.

One night at the House Group meeting, Brother Tom told us about a wonderful dream he had had several nights before. He was in his kitchen, he told us, when suddenly Jesus Himself came to the door. I'll make Him the best meal I've ever cooked, Brother Tom thought ecstatically. In his dream he set to work and soon placed before the Master a plate of grilled fish covered in cheese sauce, fluffy white potatoes and green peas. 'But,' finished Tom sadly, 'I woke up before I saw Him enjoying it.' Mrs Burton's face was a study, but Tom had not finished. 'Two days later, I had just taken my brothers their meal in the refectory, leaving my own in the oven. When I came back to fetch it, I heard a knock on the back door, and outside in the rain stood a very smelly tramp, who asked for a meal.' Communities like Brother Tom's are obliged by their rule to give hospitality, but there was no food left, except Tom's own plate in the oven.

'So rather crossly I served him with it at the kitchen table. But as I watched him begin to eat, I realised it was grilled fish in cheese sauce with potatoes and peas. I was so overwhelmed I had to start washing the saucepans to hide my tears.' 'As much as ye have done it unto one of the least of these my brothers, ye have done it unto me' (Matt. 25: 40 AV).

It so happened that John, the tramp, had recently been converted and baptised by a wonderful man, Pastor Lywood, who works tirelessly among gipsies and men of the road. Dear old John could praise the Lord even louder than Brother Tom. While he stayed on with the brothers, he started to come to our church in Mayfield. But John had a bad drinking problem, so the community had to ask him to leave, and he began sleeping rough again round the village, sheltering in farm buildings and even under hedges. Of course he did not need to, with the welfare state and many private charities, but he had been a tramp for so long, he hated the thought of being restricted.

One very cold Sunday as he sat stinking in the pew in front of us, Naomi whispered, 'Mum, let's ask him back for lunch.' We did, and he stayed with us for the rest of the day while everyone breathed through their mouths, and not through their noses, trying hard to keep remembering Tom's dream. It was easy enough for me – I'd lost my sense of smell!

When it was late and we began to make 'final noises' in John's direction, Naomi drew me into the kitchen and said, 'Mummy, you can't let us sleep in warm beds while John freezes under a hedge.' We had no room in the house so we made him a bed in the shed at the bottom of the garden where Tony hides when he wants to write a book.

'You're welcome to stay here tonight, John,' we said, and he took up permanent residence!

What a good story it would make if I could say that John reformed and became a member of AA, but sadly John likes drink too much to be delivered from it, and still frequently disappears for a few wild days, always returning repentant and needing a bath. He likes being a tramp, and also he did not get his nickname, Burglar Bill, round the village for nothing. But he has given us far, far more than we could ever have given him – a few old clothes, a shed, and his food. If we had paid him for the hours of work he does for us, Tony's salary would not be adequate. He hacked the garden back into shape, mended the drive, cleaned the car, and then quietly came along behind me doing all the things he knew by instinct I could not manage – peeling potatoes, polishing furniture, scrubbing floors and vacuuming the carpets.

'You sit down, Mrs Woman,' he would say, 'I'll do that, while you have a cupacoffee.'

The village looked at us askance and our friends gave us lectures on bad influences on the children. Even the village policeman warned us to be careful, but we just do not deserve the pure unselfish love John still gives us to this day. The Lord sent him along to be my lost strength and energy, and to teach us that 'Our God *shall* supply all our needs', even if He does so in rather unconventional ways.

## Chapter Fourteen

Once I heard a preacher say, 'Come to Jesus and all your problems will be solved.' I'm glad for him that his life was so easy, but I am beginning to think it is more a question of: 'Come to Jesus and your problems will increase but you will have Him there to help you in them.'

It was spring, and old familiar friends were beginning to reappear in the overgrown garden. The depression had gone, the Lord's presence was a reality again, and I was stronger physically as well. Everything in the garden (and the house) should have been lovely, but as I emerged from my self-centred cocoon, I realised what a hammering the children had taken over the previous year.

Duncan was now the terror of the village, the despair of his teacher, and so difficult in Sunday school that Tony had to teach him in a separate private class all on his own. My handicap embarrassed him terribly.

'Don't ever come into school,' he told me, 'I couldn't bear my friends to stare at you.'

Later when I needed sticks again, he hid them constantly. I lost five in a row and the physio department were going mad. His love of sport and vigorous movement was outraged by my lack of co-ordination.

Jane still could not seem to forgive me for deserting her, and did not want to start relying on me again – she could no longer trust me. She was as rude and morose as any teenager could be, and was also in very serious trouble at school. But Sarah was worse than any of them! She can talk about it now quite frankly, but at the time I was just baffled by her behaviour.

'When you were in hospital Dad relied on *me*. We made all the decisions together; I was in charge. I missed you, but when you came back you were not my mum any more, you were more like my great-great-grandmother. You never appreciated all I had done, you just grumbled because the kitchen was reorganised. I wanted you to look after me again, but every time we came near you it was "pick up that for me" or "reach this down". I felt guilty inside because I hated the way you looked and how I felt about you, so I freaked out.'

She certainly did! Withdrawing herself from the closeness of the family, she started mixing with a wild set of friends, going out with a non-Christian boyfriend and attending rowdy parties. She did no work at school whatever. Thank God it was not her O-level year, but the end-of-term exams were important because they decided which subjects she would be taking.

I have discovered since, from the teenage children of terminally ill or suddenly handicapped parents, that all these reactions are quite normal. But it was a real anguish at the time. I could feel them drifting away from us and from God. Tony and I prayed earnestly for them all, with fasting. 'Lord,' I cried, 'have You forgotten that night in the hospital when I said all I want is for my children to know and love You?'

We long for the very best for our children – easy, carefree lives with success and achievement – but strangely that is not the best soil for growing character or dependence on God.

I heard recently that horticulturists have discovered that causing stress to tiny seedlings by touching them regularly appears to have an effect on their growth. The plants that receive this 'harsh' treatment initially appear to be stunted. However, by the time they are ready to be planted out, they are far more sturdy than the seedlings raised in 'untroubled' conditions.

I am convinced that the same rule applies to humans.

119

James 1: 2 in the Living Bible says: 'Dear brothers, is your life full of difficulties and temptations? Then be happy, for when the way is rough, your patience has a chance to grow. So let it grow, and don't try to squirm out of your problems. For when your patience is finally in full bloom, then you will be ready for anything, strong in character, full and complete.'

Of course no parent wishes disaster on their children, and it is a real agony when *you* are the cause of their lives being unsettled. I struggled daily with a deep feeling of guilt – it was my fault that they were suffering and *I* was the reason they were behaving so badly.

Many other parents I have talked to, who are having a rough time with their teenagers, share this deep feeling of guilt. As parents we are all constantly making mistakes and failing our children in countless ways, so when they appear to go off the rails, we despairingly blame ourselves. It's this feeling of guilt that causes us to try to 'make it up to them' by being soft, which only makes matters worse. We have to ask God to deal with the guilt; I can't think why I didn't do that at the time.

In May Sarah caught a bad dose of flu, and for a week or two I put her depression down to 'post-flu blues', but as time passed I was horrified to observe her going through the ghastly experience from which I had so recently emerged. When she 'couldn't face going to school' and locked herself in her room for hours, crying, I wasted no time. I had learnt my lesson.

First I went straight to Burrswood. Sarah refused to come with me, which lowered me a notch, and then worse still, I was late for the healing service. I wanted to catch Father Keith before it began so I could tell him about Sarah, but they were singing the first hymn when I finally lurched in.

This is just a waste of time, I thought in agitation. If I could have explained to him first, he could have prayed for Sarah when he lays hands on me.

As I knelt that morning at the communion rail, something

120

wonderful happened. Father Keith put his hands on my head and prayed as usual for me and for those for whom I prayed, and then he paused, as if listening to God, then he said, 'Fear not, I am in control of this situation, it will bring Me glory, and My blessings will not cease.' I knew that was a word straight from God for us, and I went away clutching it, like a rope thrown to a drowning person.

Our doctor was marvellous. He said it was post viral depression, coupled with the strain of my illness. I felt Sarah should go straight back to school, knowing from my own past how hard it is to go back once you stop. He would not hear of it, and she spent the rest of the summer fruit-picking at a local farm.

As I have already said, living with a depressed person is terrible. I knew only too bitterly well what she was going through, but she did not want to share her world with me – she was a teenager. Jane's school troubles were escalating alarmingly, and she and Sarah were both so rude and aggressive at home, life was almost intolerable! I could not say the right thing to either of them, or to Duncan either for that matter. As usual I knew how to cope in theory, but in practice I did all the wrong things, and became just as rude and bad-tempered as they were.

'Why am I such a failure as a mother, Lord?' I wept at the kitchen sink one morning, when I had lost my temper with one of the children yet again. 'They were all so lovely when they were little, now they have rejected me utterly.'

'You said you wanted to share the fellowship of my suffering,' He replied. 'The day they dragged Me to Calvary I looked like the greatest failure of all time, and the rejection of "My own" when they received Me not, was a greater suffering than the pain of the whips. Only parents who admit they are failures and so rely on Me are successful in My sight.'

That was a real turning point. Just knowing that Jesus understands what it feels like to be rejected helped. Over the last three years, although Tony and I have been conscious so often that we have failed, we have clung to the promise in James I: 5: 'If any of you lack wisdom let him ask of God' (RSV). We have seen all those three children changing wonderfully, and each one having a definite encounter with God. As parents we long to do everything for our children, but sometimes the only thing we can do is step out of the way and let God act in their lives – healing them of consequences of our own mistakes and inadequacy.

Sarah went back completely happily to school that autumn and discovered the enjoyment of working really hard for her O-levels, but she still would not go to church with us.

'Our church bores me, and I hate sitting in the pew like all the other good little Larcombes.'

'Well, why don't you choose a church of your own, and go there as a person in your own right?' I replied. She looked slightly amazed, but replied, 'I might just do that. I'll go with Lois to her church – they have dancing in the aisles and drums there.'

She went to church with Lois, and was deeply blessed, and soon she had dragged along most of the wild set she had been mixing with earlier in the year, and one after another they found the Lord. Yes, we did miss worshipping as a whole family together, but it was only our pride that liked to see all our children with us on a Sunday. I genuinely would not mind if they all went to different churches, so long as they are all growing in the Lord.

Perhaps Jane needed to get herself into deep trouble at school in order to test us. When she discovered we loved her whatever she did, and were prepared to stand by her, she relaxed and her behaviour problems ceased. All the same, I still found her rudeness and unhelpful attitude at home often made me so angry I did not even want to pray for her. When I told the Lord about this, He said, 'Don't pray for her any more then, just praise Me for her.' That was far from easy at first, I can tell you, but as it became easier He showed me that my negative, critical attitude to her was destroying our relationship.

'But, Lord,' I said, 'there's always something to be negative and critical about.'

'You can praise *Me*, so now praise her,' He replied. Well, that was even harder, but as I exaggerated my thanks and positively buttered her with appreciation every time she did anything that was even remotely helpful, she became a great deal more responsive. The other children looked rather aggrieved at all the unusual fuss I was making of her, reminding me of the prodigal son's older brother. Meanwhile Jane blossomed with this encouragement, and has developed into a marvellous cook and a real help and joy to us, while our relationship with her is closer now than we have known it before. God is also answering our prayer for Duncan – people meeting him for the first time would never believe he was once the local terror!

By summer I felt wonderfully better, and once again we began to believe that God was healing me. That bad patch when I had first arrived home was surely just a satanic attack on our faith. Our family increased when Gom retired and came to live with us. Our house had elastic sides and fortunately she loved John as much as we did. Strangely, they have a lot in common. They both derive the maximum enjoyment from the little things of life, and they neither of them care one jot for their own comfort. Between us we ran the household, and made a blissfully happy team.

We went back to the same hostel in Yorkshire that summer and it seemed hardly possible that a whole year had gone by. I could walk without a stick and I felt positively drunk with the beauty of the scenery and the joy of feeling well.

'Next year, we'll walk the whole Pennine Way together,' I promised the family, and we bought maps and guide books in anticipation. I went into training and as soon as we got home I started a get-fit campaign. I became a complete health-food addict, and even tried to force my unco-ordinated body to jog.

That autumn was the happiest time in my whole life. The children were peaceful and settled again. Tony looked ten years younger, and because John and Gom did most of the work, I was free to do something I really wanted to do. I had written several children's books some years before, but I longed to try a novel for teenagers. My fingers could not hold a pen but in my reclusive teenage years I had taught myself to type, so I locked myself in my bedroom and tried to make a start. But it was completely impossible to write a word in our house because John and Gom never stop talking, or should I say shouting, because they are both rather deaf! I had to drive myself into the middle of a field and type on my knee in the back of the car. I used to cry with joy over the beauty of the golden leaves as I walked through the countryside with our little dog Minty. It was so easy to praise the Lord that autumn, and even the book was accepted.

Then one day I caught a little snuffly cold from the children. It was not even bad enough to keep them off school, but the effects on me were devastating. The joy of banging your head against the wall comes when you stop, but if you start again it is far worse than the first time, because you know what is coming. Once more the pain, giddiness and fatigue clamped down on me as the inflammation flared up again, and I was sent back to the neurologist I first met in London.

'Your condition seems to have reached the chronic stage,' he explained in his usual patriarchal manner. 'You now have persistent inflammation of the brain, menenges, nerves and muscles. There is nothing we can do to cure this, or reverse the damage it will do. You have been unusually lucky over the last few months, but you must expect the condition to have periods when it worsens – we call them relapses. If you keep away from infection, and really rest, you will have fewer relapses.' That struck me as a hilarious thing to say to a mother of six young children!

'Learn to enjoy the better times,' he said graciously as he showed me to the door.

How odd, I thought as I staggered out of the neurological department. 'All I can do is laugh! For sixteen months I've believed the Lord was healing me gradually. Now I find He's doing no such thing, and I don't even mind. Perhaps that is a greater miracle than my healing.' That numb feeling lasted for weeks, but it was only the mind acting as a thumb does when you hit it with a hammer. The pain is delayed, but it has to come in the end.

During that numb patch I felt almost euphorically happy. I still had my lovely peaceful home, I could see the woods and fields even if I could not walk in them, and I was carried along on the love and prayers of our little church and all our Christian friends who had become all-important to me again, since I came out of the depression.

But one Sunday afternoon a huge bombshell fell and exploded my peace completely.

## Chapter Fifteen

'I can't stand it any longer!' burst out Tony one day, as we sat on a seat while the children swarmed over the ruins of Pevensey Castle.

'Stand what?' I said blankly.

'Stand living in Mayfield, we just have to move back to Tunbridge Wells.' In my dazed state I had failed to see how worn and tired he was looking. His mind had not been numbed by the shock – he saw into the future all too clearly.

'I really cannot spend my whole life driving between Tunbridge Wells, Wadhurst and Mayfield. It's not just the swimming now, they've all got their hobbies and interests and they can't go anywhere now unless I take them. And let's face it, this house is quite unsuitable for you now, and we'll never cope with the garden again.'

'The Lord sent us John to help over that,' I put in.

'We can't rely on him,' said Tony crossly, 'he'll get himself run over one night when he's drunk.' I remembered the reason our house had not sold before and clutched at a straw.

'We'll never sell the house with all the cracks.'

'We'll have a jolly good try,' answered Tony mulishly, 'and what's more, I need a bigger church.' We had attended huge Anglican churches in Paddock Wood and Tunbridge Wells and I knew he felt happier in a larger, less intense atmosphere, but I flourished in the intimacy of something more like a house church.

We drove halfway home in silence. I was too stunned to speak. I had offered my home and friends up to the Lord at

126

Burrswood that day, but I had been so relieved when He had given them back.

'Look, we must pray about this,' I said at last, secretly hoping that God would listen to my side of the argument. We did pray, and we asked the Lord for a definite sign.

After tea that day our neighbour Charles popped in to the kitchen as we were washing up. The houses were semi-detached, but because of years of enlargements our side was much bigger than theirs.

'We were wondering if you would object to our building an extension,' he said, 'we are feeling rather cramped now with three children.'

'Don't bother to do that,' said Tony, wiping his hands on the tea towel. 'Buy our end.'

'What about the cracks?' I said desperately.

'Oh, our side has them too,' beamed Charles, 'they don't bother us, we won't even have this surveyed.'

'But you'll never sell your side if it's subsiding,' I went on doggedly.

'I'm an estate agent,' smiled Charles blandly, 'don't worry about that.'

If that wasn't the sign we had asked for, what was? But I still locked myself into the loo and cried for half an hour after he had gone.

'There is only one house in Tunbridge Wells I could ever bear to live in,' I sniffed when finally I came out, 'and that is Sally's house.' We had been to dinner with Sally some years before, and although her house was at the end of a Victorian terrace, it overlooked from every window a lovely park full of old mature trees. Next morning Tony went into an estate agency on his way to work.

'We do have a house with six bedrooms,' they said. 'Just coming on to the market today.' It sounds like one of those stories sometimes told in sermons that sound too neat and perfect to be believable, but I shan't feel the same lack of conviction now when I hear of such happenings. For that house actually *was* Sally's house! We had asked God for a sign, but he seemed to be giving us two. Tony dashed home to fetch me, and we went straight round to see it, but I was determined not to like it this time.

'It's in a road, I'll feel I'm living in a goldfish bowl,' I complained.

'We've got nothing to hide,' Tony pointed out, as we treated ourselves to a cup of coffee in a local café.

'It's wrong to move the kids, now they've just settled down.'

'Moving schools might do them all good,' Tony said firmly, and I realised we were at a complete deadlock for the first time in our married lives. There was no compromising this time. What happens when a Christian couple have this experience – who's right and who gives in?

'Look,' I said, gripping my coffee cup for support, 'Colossians 3: 15 says, "The peace that Christ gives is to guide you in the decisions you make," so surely a Christian couple like us ought to have peace over a big thing like moving house?'

'We need to pray this over with someone right away from Mayfield or Tunbridge Wells,' Tony replied. 'Let's go down to Southampton, and see Hugh and Ginny.'

Hugh O'Connor had recently given up a dental practice so that he and his wife could both devote all their time to biblical counselling. As we drove down through the fog of a November morning, I felt sure they would make Tony see reason. We prayed with them, explained our dilemma and prayed again, and then the worst happened! It was *me* who had to see reason.

'When you reach a head-on crash like this,' explained Hugh, 'it is the wife who must submit to her husband and trust God to guide them both through Him. He is answerable to God for the welfare of his family.' I had known all that for years, but it was the actual doing of it that was so hard.

'It is difficult for a man to adjust to living with a disabled wife, so you must make things as easy as possible for him.

128

Physically and spiritually, he would be better off in Tunbridge Wells.'

'But I need the peace of the country,' I burst out.

'No, Jen,' replied Ginny. 'All you need is Jesus.'

We went home and finally 'clinched the deals' with Charles and Sally. With my conscious mind I had submitted to Tony, but every single day I got myself out on two sticks to the nearest wood, and cried as if I had been bereaved.

Brother Tom discovered me in tears one day, and had no sympathy whatever.

'I'd live in a sewer if Jesus wanted me to,' he said cheerfully. That helped me so much I was fine for a few days and then drifted back into self-pity.

One sparkling frosty morning, when every dead leaf and bare twig in the wood looked as if it were covered with diamonds, I shouted out to God, 'How can You expect me to live in a town? Don't you realise all this beauty *is* You to me, not just Your creation, but a see-able feel-able *You*. I can't seem to worship You without it.'

'I know that,' He replied, 'and I made it all for you to enjoy, but now you must learn to see Me in people, not lonely beauty – in the old, sick and lonely, the depressed and tired, and love them just as you love these frosted branches.'

I wrote it all down as usual, and reading it each morning helped me for at least a month. It would not have hurt so much if we could have gone quickly, but the Lord's timing is always perfect and I really think I learnt more during the following months than at any other period of my life.

In a large church it is possible for a Christian to hide and suffer in privacy. That I think is why Tony likes a big church – he needs privacy if he is suffering. Our church was so small that there was no way we could suffer without hurting everyone else as well. When we announced that we were going to move they found it hard to understand, and some even felt we were rejecting them and all their great love and kindness to us. Tony was an elder and we had both been involved in the large Sunday school for years. Why did we have to go? Having submitted to Tony by allowing the move to be put into the pipeline, I felt it was not really playing fair not to support him in word as well as deed. So I would say brightly to my friends, 'We feel we shall all be better off in town, now I can't drive the car, and the house and situation are just not suitable now I'm disabled.'

But yet again I felt a terrible hypocrite inside for not saying how I really felt. The hammer on the thumb effect was rapidly wearing off. The shock of being permanently disabled came to me slowly, but it had to come. It is harder for a Christian to accept than it is for a person with no belief, because we know God *can* heal, so why doesn't He? I have met many disabled people over the last three years, and it is sad to note how much better-adjusted and peaceful the ones who have no faith in God so often are.

I felt deeply that our moving house was a public capitulation to the illness – a final laying aside of hope and faith, and I knew that some of the local Christians did too. I could not tell Tony how I felt after that day with Hugh and Ginny, so the hurt inside became resentment, and bitterness made communication between us virtually impossible.

Tony himself was going through a very bad time just then. In many ways it is harder to adjust to living with a disabled person than it is to be disabled yourself. The enormous physical burden of looking after six children is sometimes enough to crush two parents, but to face it alone with the added care of an invalid, and a responsible job to hold down, must sometimes feel terrifying. And then there was the frustration. For a man who has always thought and acted at high speed, it must be terrible to be chained for life to a slow-moving tortoise. I remembered what it had been like caring for my mother as well as a herd of high-speed children, and I knew how he felt, but was powerless to help.

It is also extremely hard living with someone in almost constant pain. Apart from their bad temper, they are either floating away on their painkillers or desperately trying to do without them. You can't just hug them when you feel like it in case you hurt them – though actually we would rather be hugged and hurt than not hugged at all. It's doubly hard within a marriage because it means the whole physical side can become a source of tension rather than release.

'I don't know how to help you!' Tony would explode sometimes. He could see I needed assistance dishing up a meal or pouring out the tea, but if he took over and did it for me, I felt threatened – crushed and more useless than ever. I knew without him telling me that my illness revolted him and he was frightened of how he might react in the future if it became even worse. Because I knew, I pulled away from him, hurt and humiliated, and as always when suffering he retired into a morose, silent shell that I could not penetrate. It was not that he had stopped caring about me, but both of us were imprisoned by the walls we had set up around ourselves, and we could not express our love. Once again our relationship was in very great danger.

Some time in those unhappy months I heard that Satanists are praying and fasting all over the country for the break-up of Christian marriages, and I realised suddenly that we were being attacked by the powers of darkness.

That Sunday in church someone told a Bible story for the children. It was all about how the Israelites, when they were slaves in Egypt, had to kill a lamb and paint the doorposts of their houses with its blood. The angel of death who was sent to bring destruction to Egypt passed over the houses where he saw the blood, and the families inside were safe. 'Jesus shed His blood for us, just like that lamb,' said the speaker, 'but we have to paint it on the doors of our lives if we want to be safe from the powers of darkness.'

'Perhaps we should do that for our marriage,' I said to Tony that night. We both realised we were in a state of crisis, so we knelt down and asked God to cover our marriage with the blood that Jesus had shed for us. Once under that protection we were safe from Satan's power, and although it did not seem to make any difference at the time, looking back I can see it as a turning point in our relationship.

## Chapter Sixteen

As my numbed acceptance of the disablement wore off, a desperate desire for healing and strength set in. I was beginning to fear that our family might break apart if I did not get better quickly, and I wondered how often Tony regretted giving me his cuff link. If God would only heal me all our lives could be easy and happy once again.

So I set out on a frantic search for healing. I read books, listened to tapes, visited healing services or people with a gift of healing, and of course we prayed earnestly ourselves.

Looking back, I think I stopped looking at Jesus and concentrated on my own body instead. I was forgetting that we must seek the Lord for Himself and not His gifts, or we block the very gifts He wants to give us. I wish I had remembered Oswald Chambers' words, 'God wants you in a closer relationship to Himself than receiving His gifts, He wants you to get to know Him.'

Many of our friends who attended different churches all over the district were uniting their prayers for my healing and the delay in signing the contracts for the house sale and purchase seemed to point to the wonderful fact that God did not want us to move and was going to step in and do something miraculous. But the weeks and months dragged on, and I seemed, in fact, to be getting worse.

'What's the hold-up, Lord?' I kept demanding. Could it still be Satan who was to blame? I knew from that experience in the Kent and Sussex that Jesus has given us the authority to oust him, so I went into action. I had realised some years before that evil spirits can penetrate weak places in our armour, and if unchecked can begin gradually to influence our lives. With earnest prayer and fasting I examined my life to see if there could be any spirit of infirmity, doubt or lethargy that could be causing my problems. Then, with the help of someone who has a deliverance ministry, we commanded all such enemies to be gone in the name of Jesus.

We also at that time ransacked the house for objects that could be causing harm. For some reason it was late one evening in a high wind when we finally made a huge bonfire at the bottom of the garden and Sarah threw into it all her cassettes and records made by groups who were openly Satanists. I put in books I had used for research on the occult for the teenage novel, and we even rummaged through the family museum and pulled out souvenirs from abroad such as devil masks and carved gods. I shall never forget John's incredulous face as he watched us through the window of his nearby shed – hoping no doubt that the wind would not change direction!

But still my condition was unchanged. My friends were puzzled. They could see the pain and weakness I was living with, and they had prayed for my healing, never doubting God could make me well. When He did not, they knew it was not their lack of faith or sacrificial prayer; it could not be God's fault, and so it must be mine. Many of the friends whose love and respect I depended on began to look at me oddly, and I felt them draw away from me, baffled. I suppose they felt they were wasting their time praying for me, while I continued to block my own healing. Unanswered prayer can seem very threatening to Christians.

'You don't have to suffer one more day,' beamed one friend whom I had led to the Lord a couple of years before. 'I've been reading this marvellous book, all you have to do is look to Jesus in faith.'

I could not dampen her enthusiasm by telling her I had read that book years before, and the effect of 'looking to Jesus in faith' was nearly driving me demented.

'You're a disgrace to the Lord, when you hobble round on sticks,' said another friend sternly. 'You should be demonstrating the Lord's power to make you whole.'

We went to church while visiting some friends and hugely enjoyed the free worship and lovely praising choruses, but as we left the church one of the elders came up to me and said, pointing to my surgical collar and sticks, 'You don't *have* to have those, you know.'

'I'd fall flat on my face without them,' I giggled feebly, but he was not laughing.

'Jesus could take them from you if you let Him,' he continued. 'Sometimes we cling on to illness as a way of feeling important and being noticed. Are you *willing* to be healed?'

'Am I willing, Lord?' I cried that night. 'Do people think I am some sort of hypochondriac? Perhaps I am one.'

As a child I had been delivered from school by having pneumonia or rheumatic fever; was I now escaping from life through illness again? But why should I want to escape from a life I loved so much? I could see clearly that a long-term illness could be very destructive to the personality. Was I enjoying too much the sympathy and attention I received?

I had positively shaken with rage after that man had spoken to me, but really he did me a great deal of good. That night I recognised the danger of the illness becoming the centre of my life, ruling me, becoming like an absorbing hobby.

'Lord,' I prayed, 'help me to put You in the very centre of my life, and then You can push the illness away to the circumference.' But still I could not get myself off to sleep that night. I kept thinking: Am I willing?

'Lord, I know I want to be well, but is my subconscious mind wanting to be ill? If my will is blocking your will, show me how to change it.'

Suddenly I simply had to laugh, and Tony groaned in his sleep and turned over. Worrying about your will is like trying to lift a bucket when you're standing in it, I thought. If my will belongs to the Lord, then surely it is His job to control it and make it line up with His own.

I slid cautiously out of bed and knelt down in the darkness. 'Lord,' I prayed, 'I want what You want. Please will You do all the rest.' I was soon drifting off to sleep repeating Philippians 2: 13 (AV): 'For it is God which worketh in you both to will and to do of his good pleasure.' It is not for us to 'will' and Him to 'do'. He's responsible for the whole thing, when we ask Him to be.

'I have a word from the Lord for you.' It seemed almost every day that someone came in, rang or wrote a note starting with those words. We became utterly confused because surely if they had all come from the Lord, they would not have been so contradictory.

One person said, 'The Lord wants you to fight harder.' Only the next day someone else rang to say, 'The Lord says, rest in Me, you are trying too hard.' Several people mentioned my will being the block, when both the Lord and I knew He was already dealing with that. I was beginning to feel rather hunted when another friend said, rather cryptically, 'It is your husband's attitude that is the hindrance,' but she refused to explain what she meant. When someone else waylaid me in the school car park, I really longed to be able to run away. 'It is your parents' sins that are being punished,' she said, as wintry sleet bit our cheeks. 'Or it might be your relationship with them that is causing physical harm.'

'I've had the healing of memories,' I told her tearfully, 'and my parents were the most godly people I shall ever meet. Of course they sinned, but God punished Jesus for that, not me.'

The last straw came when a Christian leader we know well and respect greatly, said, 'Jen, have you ever stopped to consider *why* so much prayer which has been offered for you has not been answered? You must search your heart.' I hardly had time to take breath before someone else came up to me and said, 'Jen, the Lord wants you to stop being so introspective.'

135

Job's comforting friends seemed to surround me, and I was beginning to want healing just to save my spiritual reputation! It was very good for my pride to know everyone was talking about me, each with their own opinion as to why I was not getting better.

The Lord certainly does give His servants messages to deliver to individuals. He was constantly doing that in the Bible, and He still does it now, but we have to make sure it is not just our own critical feelings we are voicing. God can also give us a burden to go and lay hands on someone for healing, but again we have to be careful it really is His prompting, and not our own enthusiasm, or untold damage can be done to the sick person's faith. When we feel the urge to speak or heal, it need not take hours of waiting on the Lord first, we only have to stop and mentally turn to Him for guidance. But if we ask the Lord to stop us from making a mistake, He most certainly will.

I wanted to be well so badly I twisted myself into mental and spiritual knots, trying to take all this conflicting advice. So it seemed a positive relief when someone said, 'Stop praying for healing – just praise the Lord.' Her face radiated confidence. I had read many books on praise, so when she added, 'Praise always brings results,' something pricked me at the back of my mind. I took her advice enthusiastically, but the pricking grew worse, until I faced the fact that praise, when used as a means to an end, becomes a ghastly form of flattery – buttering up God to get our own will done.

Surely, I thought in desperation, we should be able to praise God whether He brings us good or bad, and go on praising Him even when our circumstances do not change (Job 2: 10). Oswald Chambers said, 'We must not use God like a machine for blessing men.'

But the pressure to be healed increased both within myself and from the people around me, and when I was told that a young man from our fellowship had lost his newly found faith because God had not answered his earnest prayers for me, I felt miserable and condemned. The feeling grew when I realised the church youth group were giving themselves to prayer for me, and my healing was becoming terribly important to their faith.

My greatest comfort was the book of Job. I could identify with him perfectly. Like him, I had lost my possessions (home), health, relationship with my husband and my spiritual standing and status. Of course I should not have minded what people thought of me, but I did!

The strain of all this conflict was too much, and it erupted violently one Saturday morning. I was confined indoors when I would much rather have been in the woods with the children, facing a huge pile of ironing I did not have the physical strength to do. Tony made some bright remark about how convenient it was going to be living in town, and something inside me snapped. All the pent-up bitterness over the loss of my fields and lanes burst uncontrollably, and picking up my steaming iron, I flung it in his direction. Fortunately it missed, hit the wall and smashed, letting off steam as it died.

'It'll cost at least fifteen pounds to buy a new one,' remarked Tony with maddening detachment. Making sure the children were out of range, I really told him what I thought of him, giving vent to the torrent of words I had buried for weeks, but suddenly I was halted in mid-sentence.

'What's the matter?' I faltered in panic as I saw him huddled in his chair, clutching his chest, his twisted face a ghastly colour.

'It'll pass in a minute,' he gasped, 'they always do.'

'What do you mean, they always do?' I demanded, suddenly realising how very much I loved him. When he could speak again, he told me he had been having severe chest pains for some time, but had not liked to worry me with them. After a cup of tea he looked better, but I made him promise to visit the doctor on Monday.

I just had to be alone with God that afternoon, and I forced myself across the fields to the woods, but the heavy March rain had turned the path into a muddy bog, and soon my wellington boots were helplessly stuck and I burst into tears. 'This path is just what our lives have turned into,' I told the Lord as I sat down heavily in a puddle. 'It's just a squelchy mess.'

'I know,' He replied, 'but keep on remembering that I am right here in the mess with you.' The memory of that muddy path has helped me so often since.

Next morning in church I was still rocking with the shock and more desperate than ever to be healed. If Tony suddenly died of a heart attack, I had to be fit to care for the children. When all the Sunday school had gone out halfway through the service – and of course Tony with them, to teach his huge class consisting of Duncan – Brian suddenly said publicly, 'Jen, the elders and I would like to pray for your healing right now.'

'This is the moment at last!' I thought as I went happily to the front of the church. I was secretly pleased that Tony was safely out of the way. Watching my frenzied attempts to take everyone's conflicting advice had worried him – though typically, he had made no comment. His trust in God's ability to do what was best for us all was much greater than mine, but of course I did not realise that at the time. I just thought that if he was in church his apparent lack of faith might spoil the elders' prayer! As they gathered round me praying, I added silently, Lord, please heal Tony as well.

But by the following Sunday Tony had an appointment to see the heart specialist, and I was having such a bad relapse I could not even go to church, but lay in bed miserably wondering how many young people's faith I was damaging by this latest public failure.

That week there was a mini mission being held in the district by a very remarkable woman. Over the two years she had been a Christian, God had done wonderful things for her and she longed to pass them on. She happened to be visiting our church that particular Sunday. She was furious with Satan for his hold over me, and positively stamped round to our house straight after the service. For two exhausting hours she prayed with me and drove out yet more spirits that might still be causing my defeat, while I tried not to hear the chaos of Tony dishing up the Sunday lunch in the kitchen beneath us.

During the week she was to hold two coffee mornings, and I was determined not to miss either. The first was on Tuesday, and the house where it was held seemed to be packed with people when I finally crawled in. She talked for an hour, and all she said about healing was right. She used verse after verse from the Bible and we all had it down in black and white before us.

'It is God's will,' she said, looking round the room with her compelling dark eyes, 'for *all* his children to live in health and financial freedom. In the Old Testament healing and prosperity always come after repentance and obedience, and ninety per cent of the ministry of Jesus was healing the sick.'

Deep down in my mind something nagged at me. We live in an age where health, physical fitness and financial achievements are worshipped. By laying such a passionate emphasis on the gift of healing and deliberately blinding ourselves to so much else that is in the Bible, are we not just following the world's obsession with bodily perfection? The memory of the face of an old lady we had recently met flashed into my mind. A beautiful face, but it had been etched by years of pain and suffering. 'Remember, my dears,' she had told us, 'look *forward* to your inheritance (1 Peter 1). He's keeping it for you carefully in Heaven, so be glad!' We had looked up 1 Peter 1 later, not really being sure what she meant. 'We look forward to possessing the rich blessings that God keeps for His people. Be glad . . . even though it may be necessary for you to be sad for a while because of the many kinds of trials you suffer. Their purpose is to prove that your faith is genuine. Even gold . . . is tested by fire; and so your faith . . . must be tested so that it may endure' (1 Peter 1: 4–7). I groped my way to the passage again, as my confusion mounted. How can our faith be tested if all our problems

139

both physical and financial are removed from us – wouldn't we be like spoilt children?

'One of God's signs of approval is material prosperity, which of course includes health.' The voice jerked me back into the room again, back from a past generation who felt it was a privilege to suffer, right into the middle of a modern trend which was beginning to lay too much emphasis on only one side of the truth. Peter said we were assured of our inheritance in Heaven, but did that really guarantee material benefits down here as well?

'I believe God wants to demonstrate His power by physical healing this morning,' concluded the speaker, and suddenly I was conscious of everyone in the room looking at me. They all knew me and had prayed so long for me, and as I was the only ill person there it seemed obvious to them all that God's power was going to be demonstrated on me.

'I am going to put this chair here in the centre of the circle and, Jen, I want you to come and sit here while some of us lay hands on you.'

But suddenly I could not take any more. The elders of our church had prayed publicly for me not ten days before, the speaker had spent two embarrassing hours praying for me on Sunday, and I had had so many hands laid on me it was a wonder I was not bald!

Everyone sat round the room expectant and excited, but I just could not take another public humiliation.

'No,' I said, 'I won't.' A stunned shock wave circled the room.

'Don't you want God to heal you?' she demanded.

'Of course I do,' I almost wailed. 'But I feel completely confused. I agree with everything you have said this morning about God's ability to heal, but you've only quoted one side of what the Bible says. Paul had a painful physical ailment, a thorn in the flesh, but God did not heal him.'

'That is just a bad translation, he's talking of a spiritual thorn, not a physical one,' she replied.

'But Jesus said, "In the world *ye shall have* tribulation."'

'Yes, but that means persecution,' was the reply, 'not sickness.'

'What about Job then?' I quavered. 'God allowed him to be ill.'

'Job lived in a different dispensation.'

Everyone in that room was looking at me in dazed horror. I am still so embarrassed as I write about it, even my feet are turning red! I ought to have subsided, and just let them lay hands on me once again, but somehow the torrent inside me could not be dammed.

'Listen,' I was almost crying with rage by that time, 'the Bible says hundreds more things about suffering and healing, they can't all be contradictory. We can prove almost any theory we like by separate verses or illustrations. Surely each Christian must seek God's face separately to discover what is God's will for *him*. I am beginning to think that's what I should be doing instead of trying to force God to do what may only *seem* to be the best thing.'

I looked round at the shocked faces through a blur of tears.

'We can't use our faith like a demand note to wave in God's face. He treats us all as individuals, and even David Watson with all his faith and purity died of cancer!'

There is no way that you can leave with dignity when you walk like a drunken sailor, but I had hardly staggered down the garden path, when my rage died down into humiliation. How could I have lost my cool like that – all those people in that room must totally despise me. Perhaps they did not, but God allowed me to feel that they did in order to teach me that I valued other people's opinions more highly than I valued His.

As I made myself a cup of tea in the shelter of my own kitchen, I began to worry in case my negative attitude had prevented the Lord from doing for other people what he was fully able and willing to do. I felt so wretched I went back and apologised to the speaker and her hostess for ruining the coffee morning. They were very kind and loving but I still felt deeply embarrassed.

141

That night I was putting Duncan to bed and kneeling on the floor fumbling to undo a knot in his trainer laces. Seeing me on my knees, I suppose the Lord felt He could speak to me at last, and while Duncan put on his pyjamas, God said, 'You are blinded by arrogant pride. There are things in you that displease me. I must eradicate them at all costs, they are blocking your progress.'

Duncan got into bed and started drawing pictures, quite unconscious that I was still kneeling by the chair.

'Yes, Lord,' I said at last, 'do eradicate them, please, however much it hurts. I do love You and You know all I want to do is grow closer to You.'

The next day I was to have a very special treat. My friend Trish was recovering from a cancer operation. Leaving her seven children, she was coming to spend twenty-four precious hours with me. It was so good to have someone from the other side of London with whom to talk over the whole of my muddle, and better still to pray together. We sat comfortably either side of a roaring fire, talking to the Lord about our husbands and thirteen children in companionable detail, when suddenly I felt the Lord so close to us I just had to slide out of my armchair and on to my knees.

'Lord,' I cried urgently, 'show me the blockage You told me was there.'

'It is your rebellion towards Tony,' came the answer at once. 'You have submitted to him in word and deed, but not in your heart. Your rebellion has caused him actual physical pain, and you have also hurt Me by your lack of trust.'

With Trish's help I repented and asked God to change me, and as Trish and I wept and prayed together, I realised what a fool I had been to put fields and woods before my happy relationship with Tony. Worse still, I knew I had hurt the Lord.

'Whatever do I do now, Trish?' I said as we started on a new box of tissues.

'Well, you'll have to put things right with Tony,' said Trish.

142

'But he's away for a whole week, and I can't do that sort of thing over the phone,' I gulped.

'Let's have a look at James 5 and ask the Lord to show us why your elders' prayers were not answered.'

We both sat with our Bibles on our knees and looked at verses 14, 15 and 16.

'Look,' said my wise friend, 'it says you must confess your sins to one another, "so that you will be healed". If you were still rebelling inwardly, you were blocking the healing – and it says *you* call the elders, it is not for them to call you.'

'It would be a bit difficult for me to ask them to come here,' I admitted, 'because Tony is so fed up with the whole subject he won't even talk about it.'

'Look,' said Trish firmly, 'your body belongs to Tony, under God, and so you should never have consented to be prayed for without his presence and permission, and you tell me he wasn't even in church! That was part of your rebellion. It has to be Tony who calls the elders, and look,' she added, jabbing her Bible with an excited finger, 'it says there should be oil, and I'm also afraid it is quite clear that you have to confess your sins not only to Tony, but also to the elders.'

With this unpleasant thought she left me, and as I waved her away down the lane, all I could hear was my father saying, 'If you have to do something unpleasant – do it *now*!'

## Chapter Seventeen

I lay on my bed with the duvet firmly pulled over my face. I had cried for so many hours that night that even the duck down was soggy.

I had done the 'unpleasant thing' the previous evening, but if I had known it was going to be that unpleasant I would never have summoned the courage to go and confess to Brian the rebellion as Trish had said I must.

'I don't think it is only rebellion that is blocking your spiritual life,' Brian had said as I faced him over the polished expanse of his empty dining table. After half an hour with him seeing myself through his eyes, I felt like a snail without a shell. What he said would not have stung so much if I had not realised he was so painfully right! It cannot be much fun being a pastor and having the solemn responsibility of speaking the truth, but I shall be grateful to him for the rest of my life for those thirty minutes. As Psalm 19: 12 says, 'No one can see his own errors; deliver me, Lord, from hidden faults! Keep me safe, also, from wilful sins.'

For months I had been grappling with the 'wilful sins' but there are so many faults we hide under apparent 'good' things, that we even deceive ourselves, and only someone very wise and courageous can help us to 'see our own errors'. Brian had to use his surgeon's knife to reach very deep-seated poison, and he did me more good with it than any amount of soothing ointment. But as I lay there in the dark I was definitely suffering from post-operative shock! Reduced to nothing as I was in my own sight and other people's, however could the Lord go on loving such a failure? I wanted to run away and never again see anyone I had ever known.

Some time long before morning I poked my head out from under the duvet and groped for my black book. 'Whatever shall I do, Lord?' I scrawled right across the page. 'Everyone else has a word from you about my situation – except me!' Even as I wrote that I realised I had never taken the time to ask Him for one. I had spent months listening to other people's opinion and taking their conflicting advice, until I felt I had no personality or confidence left. Never once did I doubt the Lord's desire and ability to heal me. I felt it was all my own fault that I was ill.

As I saturated yet another tissue, I realised the Lord wanted to forgive and change me, if I would only give Him the chance. All this mental churning certainly was not His will; He had promised me His peace (John 14: 27). 'If only Tony was here,' I sniffed as I looked at his empty cold side of the bed.

Then I realised what a wonderful thing it was that Tony was away at a maths conference for the next seven days. Suppose I used that time to seek the Lord's face finally over this whole question? I wouldn't answer the phone or door bell, and only do the essential jobs in the house. I could even fast with Gom and Tony out of the way, so I would be more responsive to what the Lord would say.

As I slid out of bed on to my knees, I prayed the last two verses of Psalm 139. 'Examine me, Oh God and know my mind; test me and discover my thoughts. Find out if there is any evil in me and guide me in the everlasting way.' Suddenly I felt Him speaking to me through the lonely darkness.

'You have been like a tiny boat in a storm, buffeted this way and that by the opinions of others. I will make you like a firm rock in the ocean standing solidly against the waves' (James 1: 6).

That week would have been horrid enough without the icy March winds penetrating every crack in the house. I was so cold without any food inside me, I spent most of the time in bed packed round with hot-water bottles – a woolly hat on my head, an open Bible on my knee and a pencil and note book ready to write down the blocks as the Holy Spirit revealed them to me. I laugh now every time I think of it, but I did not laugh then. I felt like a huge mountain with a cave running right to its centre. If I wanted God right there in the very middle of me, I had to allow Him to dynamite His way through the granite boulders that had blocked the cave, and those explosions hurt! But I knew great peace as He identified and removed them one by one, because of His wonderful power to forgive.

'But please reprogramme my personality, Lord; don't just let me slip back into being me again,' I implored.

'I shall go on doing that for the rest of your life,' He replied. 'We shall fight a constant battle with these lumps of rock.'

'But that means I shall never be ready to be healed,' I cried.

'You can't earn your healing any more than you can earn your salvation. Both are free gifts from Me,' He replied. 'You have no more right to healing than any of the other gifts I shower on you each day, most of which you never even notice.'

In spite of the cold and hunger it was a very wonderful week, rather like a major internal spring-clean and redecoration! It was not just asking for His forgiveness. I had some practical homework as well. There were relationships He wanted me to restore, and attitudes that had to be changed. The Bible on my lap was replaced by my typewriter, as I wrote many letters. I had drawn away from so many people because I felt they despised me, but that had not pleased God. I had to reopen the relationship by making the first move – just a friendly note or card. I also had to ask forgiveness of some people I had hurt and they responded so warmly and lovingly. I also had to forgive the people who had hurt me. I needed so much help from the Lord over that,

146

but He showed me definitely that He could not forgive me unless I forgave them (Matthew 6: 14, 15). I certainly did not tell them I was forgiving them – that might have hurt them unnecessarily.

I felt massively better when all that was done, so I settled down to earnest prayer, asking the Lord how He really wanted me to pray. I knew it was no good pleading for healing and then tacking 'if it be Thy will' on to the end like a feeble failsafe. He wants us to pray specifically and with confidence. But we had never really taken the time to ask Him to tell us what He wanted to do.

'Lord,' I prayed, 'give me the gift of faith so that we can "ask in faith, nothing wavering. For he that wavereth is like a wave of the sea driven with the wind and tossed"' (James 1: 6 AV).

I had to sit there and listen to God – which is probably the most important form of prayer anyway – but I am such a gas bag I'd never realised it before. But the Lord was strangely silent, so I began to search the Bible for what He wanted me to understand.

I looked up all the different ways Jesus healed people in the gospels, searching for some common key, but I could not find one. Sometimes He connected sin with sickness as in Luke 5 and John 5, and sometimes He separated them – John 9. Why did He choose to heal that one man at the pool of Bethesda who did not even ask for His help? He had to step over a multitude of blind, lame and paralysed people to reach him, and He walked away leaving them just as they were, yet He had the power to heal them all.

I began to realise just how much Satan hates the ministry of healing because it brings such glory to God. When he cannot hinder it by doubt and unbelief, he causes us to become *too* obsessed by it. He can then use it to turn our energies away from praying for our friends who need God or taking them to meetings where they might find Him. Instead, Christians flock to healing services to have their sore toes or backaches dealt with because Satan would much

147

rather we used God as a bottle of aspirin than the answer to a lost world.

I think this is what happened at Capernaum. Jesus delivered a demon-possessed man in the synagogue (Mark 1: 23–27) and then healed Peter's mother-in-law. By evening the whole district had heard the news, and they all arrived at his door bringing everyone who was sick, and Jesus healed them. But the townsfolk were very upset when they found He was missing next morning, and Peter and his friends were sent off to find Him.

'I must preach in other towns,' Jesus said, 'that is why I came.' But His mission was thwarted when He healed a man of leprosy. 'Don't tell anyone about this,' Jesus told him sternly (verse 44), but the man 'spread the news about everywhere' (verse 45) so that Jesus could not go into the cities He longed to reach, but had to wait in the desert for people to come to Him.

When He went back to Capernaum, the crowds packed the house so tightly that men ripped open the roof to let down a man for healing, but Jesus knew the man was much more worried by his spiritual problems than his physical ones, and He said, 'Your sins are forgiven you.'

It was probably months later when He was again in Capernaum that a huge crowd ran Him to earth, and He said to them (John 6: 26): 'You are looking for me because you ate the bread and had all you wanted, not because you understood my miracles.' When He went on to say, 'I am the bread of life' (verse 35) the Jews murmured at Him (41). They did not like Him to talk about spiritual things, and verse 66 says, 'Because of this, many of Jesus's followers turned back and would not go with Him any more.'

Of course Jesus used miracles to build faith, but they were a means to an end, and not an end in themselves. It was the preaching of the Good News about the Kingdom of God that was His primary mission (Mark 1: 38).

He told Pilate (John 18: 36) that 'My Kingdom does not belong to this world.' Of course He cares intensely about our health and welfare, but He also knows how short our lives are, and how many wonderful things He is planning for our real lives with Him in eternity.

Satan also revels in confusion. So many people have said to me, 'I just don't know what I think about healing any more. Some people are healed and some are not. Why?' Whole churches waver in doubt when they have prayed earnestly for someone who has died instead of recovering. Satan tells them he has triumphed and they just don't see that person as perfectly whole at last.

Of course God does not want us to be muddled and confused, but He just cannot trust us with all the answers yet. Real faith grows when *we* don't know why, but are sure that *He* does. The Lord once said to Helen Roseveare, 'Can you trust me in this, even if I *never* tell you why?'

On the last hungry day of the week, I had to confess that even though the Lord had done so many wonderful things for me, He had not given me any particular scripture, only the conviction that mere bodily healing is not half so important in the light of eternity as our generation believes it to be.

But I was still left with that command in James 5.

'Lord, You know how uptight Tony is feeling about all this,' I prayed just an hour before he was due home. 'Please Lord, help him to share my conviction that we should call the elders in obedience to these verses. You haven't told me how You want me to pray, but I'll leave that to them, and I promise once those elders have come, I will never nag You again about healing.'

As soon as Tony's car turned into the drive, I longed to blurt out to him all that had happened to me that week, and also to get the rebellion matter off my chest quickly. However with all the children talking at once, and Gom and John joining in loudly, I realised I would have to wait.

'I've got to drive down to Bournemouth tomorrow,' Tony shouted over the din, 'come with me, and I'll take you out to lunch.' There was my chance.

I felt a terrible fool telling Tony how I felt, but I sensed he understood, as he quietly squeezed my hand. Then he began to talk, and I suddenly realised just how very hard these last few years had been for him. I also saw how deep his relationship with God had actually become. While my emotions had been vacillating between euphoria and depression via anger and doubt, he had silently plodded on towards God. How easy it is to misjudge people spiritually. It isn't necessarily those people who are always 'talking big' who are growing the most, but neither I nor some of our local Christian friends had understood this.

'Would you mind if we did a James 5 and asked the elders to come round one day soon?' I asked nervously as we began our journey home. Tony said he did not mind a bit, but first there were a few relationships and hurts he had to restore and mend himself! The wave of relief that enveloped me showed just how much hope I had pinned on those three verses.

The following Saturday morning when the elders were due to come, I woke early with a tremendous feeling of excitement. Nothing after today would ever be the same again. I knew that all over the country our friends were concentrating their prayers upon us, some were even fasting, and when we showed the four men into our lounge I knew all the children were praying upstairs.

As they stood around us both in a ring I felt utterly surrounded by love. I never shall forget Brian's face. I could not help thinking how like the Lord he was – he had seen so clearly all the nasty side of me, and yet he still loved me! We had done everything we possibly could to make ourselves ready for healing, yet we both knew we were still unworthy of seeing a miracle. We offered Him again everything we possessed, but still knew that could not buy automatic blessing.

'Nothing in my hand I bring, simply to Thy cross I cling,' I whispered as they put their hands on our heads. We asked for three things: healing for Tony, and for me, and inwardly we prayed for our marriage. I knew that moment was deeply significant in our lives.

Over the next few weeks all those prayers were answered. Tony went to the Kent and Sussex Hospital for all kinds of tests and they pronounced him to be one hundred per cent fit. We both went to Hildenborough Hall for a Christian Marriage Weekend led by Dave and Joyce Ames, and we were able to talk and pray through all our conflicts and anxieties. The Lord did heal our relationship completely, and gave us a new and deeper than ever love for each other.

Daily I seemed to grow stronger and was able to cope with moving house, unpacking tea chests, painting the kitchen and even planting some seeds in our tiny backyard.

The strangest thing of all was that I discovered, within hours of arriving in Tunbridge Wells, that Tony and the Lord had been right all along. It is just perfect for us all here, and I have never suffered one moment's doubt about leaving Mayfield.

It seems like a very specially loving present from God to have Auntie Gerry living just nearby. She moved down to Tunbridge Wells to be nearer her own family as well as all of us. Now she is here as another much-loved granny to the children and steps into the breach with total efficiency whenever there is a crisis.

But life isn't like a fairy story where people live happily ever after, nor is this a book about people who lived victoriously through difficult experiences and came out on the other side with all their questions answered. It doesn't seem as though there are any neat and tidy endings this side of Heaven.

## Chapter Eighteen

Diseases that grow steadily better, or even steadily worse, are easier to cope with than the endless ups and downs of remission and relapse. Each remission brings fresh hope for the future, which is dashed by the following relapse.

The woods have seemed very dark and bleak indeed during the last twelve months. I have had to be away from the family for long stretches of that time, either in hospital or convalescing. It has been the longest-lasting and worst relapse ever.

The Lord asked me three years ago if I could still praise Him in the wintry woods, and to be honest I don't really think I can – not if praise means a constant loud bubbling exuberance. But I am not sure that it does. Psalm 34: 1 in the Living Bible says, 'I *will* praise the Lord whatever happens.' Perhaps praising the Lord has as little connection with emotions as love has. It is an act of the will, an attitude of mind. Once, during that House Group meeting three years ago, God said to me, 'I do not want automatic praise which costs nothing. I want you to learn to praise Me when you are depressed, tempted or not having your prayers answered. That is when your praise and worship mean something to Me.' Maybe praise is just an acknowledgment that He knows what He is doing even if I don't.

A few months ago I was in hospital in London. It was the day I was officially registered disabled. Not a great boost for the morale, I can assure you! My worst fears were realised and I knew that this time I would not be able to go home and force myself to run my own household. I could not even bathe or dress myself or go anywhere except in a wheelchair. I did not feel like a person any more, just a DHSS number.

'Lord,' I whispered as I gazed hopelessly at the wall. 'You know I am a doing, going, giving person. I will never learn to be just a receiver.'

Then I glanced down at the book on my lap which George had sent me, and three words exploded in my face: 'As You did'. It was Sister Basilea Schlink's *The Blessings of Illness*, and this is the sentence that contained them: 'My Jesus, I will humbly allow others to help me, as You did.'

Surely, I thought, He was the greatest 'doer', 'goer', and 'giver' of all time. He 'came not to be ministered unto but to minister'. Then I realised in a flash that He had been dependent on others nearly all his life. He was born in someone else's stable, buried in someone else's tomb, rode on a borrowed donkey and ate His last supper in another man's house. He and His followers had been supported financially by wealthy women (Luke 8: 3), and He was even gracious enough to receive a little boy's picnic lunch.

'If you want to share the fellowship of My suffering you must learn to receive in grateful humility,' He told me gently. 'And when it hurts, hand it back to Me as an offering, which I will use to bless the people who are giving to you' (1 Chron. 11: 17, 18).

Well, I have to confess it has not hurt as much as I thought it would. Marilyn left Burrswood and looked after us for a time. Now, with the help of Lyn, the Kent County Council home help, not to mention Gom and John, we all get along hilariously, while the occupational therapists are reorganising the house with ramps, rails and a lift to make things easier in the future.

One day I received a letter from someone I had never met. Only the day before I had tearfully realised I could no longer use my typewriter. 'I feel the Lord wants me to send you this cheque so you can buy an electric typewriter,' the letter said. Tony went straight out and bought me a specially adapted model which I can even operate while lying down, and the very next day I began to write this book.

Of course the black patches still come, and one week the pain and weakness were not helped by three different friends visiting me with new theories about why I was not healed. All the old doubt and uncertainty returned, just when I thought I had conquered them once and for all. Every time I looked out of the window, I saw healthy mothers playing games with their children in the park and real, painful jealousy knifed me below the belt. So I deliberately looked out of the windows facing the road and not the park, only to see a neighbour driving off to freedom in her little mini car; the doctor had said I would never drive again. Self-pity sneaked up behind me, and the walls of my own home closed in on me like a dungeon. Lyn's cheery voice in the distance, as she did all the jobs I once thought I hated doing, did not help at all. I would have given anything just to clean the loo again, or scrub the kitchen floor.

That night I went to bed, but soon realised it was going to be one of those nights when the pain gets the upper hand. Usually I find pain brings the Lord Jesus nearer to me, because I know for sure that He understands how I feel and sits beside my bed, hurting with me. I also find prayer is easiest then, because when I am in pain, I seem extra sensitive to the many people who are suffering too in different ways, and I chat to the Lord about them, and even picture us both visiting them together in their homes, hospitals or prisons.

Once, in my active Martha days, I had said, 'To work is to pray,' as I hurtled round doing things for people. Now I can't even do much for myself, and I have turned that motto on its head: 'To pray is to work'. It is not just a form of relaxation to me now, it is an exciting professional job and I am learning as the Lord's apprentice.

But that night He seemed so far away, and I was still plagued by the unresolved emotions of the week. When the pain reached a level I could not handle I groped for my store of powerful drugs the pain clinic prescribe for occasions like that one. While I waited for them to act, I opened my Bible and chanced to read Romans 10: 12–13: 'God . . . richly blesses all who call to Him . . . everyone who calls out to the Lord for help will be saved.'

'All right, Lord – I'm calling,' I muttered, 'I just can't cope with my feelings or this pain.'

Our bedroom is a bit like Spaghetti Junction in the mornings, and I was still feeling rather vulnerable as I sipped my first cup of tea next morning. Richard sat in bed beside me reading his school reading book, Tony and Sarah sat on the far side of him in deep conversation about her A-level geography syllabus, Justyn wanted some money (as usual), and Duncan was playing me his latest Pink Floyd tape while Jane 'punked' her hair at my dressing table. Naomi had brought her breakfast up on a tray, 'just in case I was lonely!' The tears trickled out of the corners of my eyes – what a failure I was as a mother, I could not even cook them some porridge.

'Don't be silly, Mummy,' said Sarah briskly. 'We all like you best this way. Once you were always dashing about, and so busy we could never talk to you, now you're always home and ready to listen to us.'

I looked round at them all and suddenly realised they had each made a definite commitment to God, and were reading the Bible and praying each day. Surely that is what I had wanted most of all that night in hospital. Yes, they do have to do much more to help at home than other children, but strangely that has built their self-esteem because they know we rely on them, and could not cope without their help.

I don't have to strive to *do* things any more in order to be loved. My family love me for what I *am* and not just for what I do for them – and the same applies to the Lord! But it has taken me forty-two years to learn that.

The noise around me increased to a crescendo and then, quite suddenly, the Lord was speaking to me as well.

'I want you *daily* to take up your cross and follow me,' He said.

'But what do you really mean by that, Lord?' I asked Him, as I turned Richard's page, gave Justyn fifty pence and told Duncan to turn the volume down a little. Inside my head I could see a horrid picture of myself struggling like a martyr, in agony under the exhausting weight of the cross, but the Lord cut sharply across that image.

'It was like that for Me, but not for you. Your cross is a symbol of victory, you must take it up in triumph. I know you cannot handle these feelings of jealousy, doubt, self-pity and despair, but when they come take up your cross and hold it out between them and your mind. "*In* all these things you are more than conquerors"' (Rom. 8: 37 RSV). I tried it and it works!

While it is only honest to say that this last year has not been easy, it is also true to say that all eight of us have received a very real peace. Of course that peace is attacked sometimes – as I have just described. But we are not striving after something all the time and wondering, 'Is God going to heal at this service or through this person? It is *not* that we have given up hope or given in to the disease and stopped fighting, but rather that God has pushed that physical part of life into the background and filled our time with so much that is enjoyable and lovely. Life *is* fun once again; three years ago I would never have believed such a miracle was possible! After all, life really does not consist of what you can do, or what you have. It's how you feel deep inside that counts.

This peace makes talking about the Lord easier than it ever has been before. When I used to chat to people about Him in supermarket queues or at the school gate, I often became conscious of an odd expression creeping into their eyes.

It's all very well for her to talk, I could almost hear them thinking. Happily married – six healthy children – nice home – good health. If she had my problems she wouldn't talk so glibly about God's goodness.

156

I never observe that look in people's eyes now. They can see I am handicapped, and responding to my smile they soon start to chat, and I find they are hungry for God. In a world that seeks happiness in health, wealth and achievements they are fascinated to find it in someone who obviously does not have these things that the world so highly prizes. Underneath their gleaming veneer, people feel very frightened – their jobs are insecure, their marriage unstable or even finished – they fear the bomb, cancer and old age, while depression is an epidemic. To find that God gives joy and peace *in* these things, as well as release from them, fascinates people, and they will listen to me simply because I am disabled. I no longer constitute a threat as I must have done in my bossy Martha days.

Then, I probably wanted to serve God for the wrong motives. But since I have realised how completely He identifies with us in our difficulties I am beginning to see that He also wants us to identify with *Him* in *His* sufferings. Jesus did not stop suffering when He dismissed His spirit that day on Calvary. Because He loves us He will go on being hurt until the last one He loves is free of pain. Jesus wept when He saw the anguish of Mary and Martha (John 11: 33, 35). He still weeps now when tragedies devastate His people. We expect Him to ease our pain, but how can we ease His? If we really love Him we long to do so. He has no hands now to comfort and show practical love, no visible face to smile and reassure – He relies on us to be His physical body. So we serve Him to give Him pleasure – not to earn our salvation, curry His favour or boost our own morale. When he sees people He loves comforted and helped He shares their joy just as surely as He felt their pain.

The other day Gom took me back to Firtoll woods to see the bluebells and the sun playing down through the new green beech leaves. I could not help remembering that gloomy winter day when I had stood here before. Eunja's dream had not come true, yet she had prayed earnestly before she rang me, believing that God wanted her to tell me

157

about the dream. Why had God allowed me to be frightened like that?

When I returned home I looked up all the Bible references to dreams and was astonished by how many there were. It does seem that God uses dreams to communicate with people both in the Old and New Testaments. I don't know why He allowed that dream, but one thing I do know is that it blessed me. I had never considered death before – young, strong and happy people seldom do. But everyone needs to be pulled up short at some time and forced to consider how they feel about dying. I might never have faced the issue without Eunja's dream.

Through that experience I did discover that Christians have no need to fear death, and when they reach the actual point of dying it can be a glorious experience. Over the last three years I have met numerous people who are afraid to die, but in Hebrews 2: 14 we are told that 'Through His death Jesus destroyed the Devil who has the power over death, and in this way set free those who were slaves all their lives because of their fear of death.'

This generation fears death and illness above anything. Many Christians follow this trend and become obsessed with the healing God undoubtedly can give us. I've noticed that the people who are most preoccupied by the healing ministry are often those who in life most fear death and detest illness.

When Christians insist that the death of a much-prayed-for sick person is Satan's triumph, it can imply that the worst that can happen to us is death. I don't believe that any more. For a Christian, death is the beginning of everything that is lovely, and the shorter our lives, the sooner we can taste the glories of eternity. Of course it is tragic when we have to leave behind us people we love, but again we have to trust God to look after them better than we ever could.

F. B. Meyer once wrote, 'It is given to some to teach, others to work and some to suffer as a ministry.' That's a very unpopular idea these days, now that the ministry of healing, having lain largely dormant for centuries, is being revived by God. Only the deliberately blind can deny the miracles that are happening, but why must we claim that it is *always* God's will for his children to be physically well in this life? I believe that Satan has brought this heresy into our thinking today, and he is using it to crush and discourage many who believe without a doubt that God can heal, and who would fifty years ago have been radiant in the joy of discovering that His 'strength is made perfect in weakness'.

F. B. Meyer went on to say, 'The child of God is often called to suffer because nothing will convince onlookers of the reality and power of true religion as suffering will do, when it is borne with Christian resignation and fortitude.' In these days of body worship, are we not forgetting that 'My strength shows up best in weak people'? Could not God sometimes be glorified *more* by helping a person in an illness than by removing it?

Suffering seems to give Christians the opportunity to grow spiritually more than anything else. By trying to oust suffering from the 'victorious Christian life' we risk spiritual immaturity. There are no pain-free short cuts to growth – though Satan would have us think there are.

These days we make God too small. We think that if we rub Him in the right way, like Aladdin's lamp, He will lavish on us anything we ask for, and remove all problems from our lives. We live in an age of stereotypes but God, who made each blade of grass different, is the God of the individual. We read a book or hear a talk by someone to whom God has given a special blessing, gift or healing, and we feel like second-class citizens when He does not do exactly the same for us. But He could not treat us all the same when He made us different.

Every time I have a remission, I am convinced that the Lord has healed me for good, and every time I have a relapse the same old depression washes in. But I wanted to write this book while I still don't know all the answers, because I think that all too often we pretend to other people that we're in a constant state of victory partly to convince ourselves. To me, it's better to admit that we are often bewildered and muddled up inside even when we *know* that God is in control. That tension is always there, and I think that it's intrinsic to our faith.

Psalm 73 says, 'What else have I in Heaven but you? Since I have you, what else could I want on earth? My mind and my body may grow weak, but God is my strength. He is all I ever need . . . But as for me, how wonderful to be near God . . . and to proclaim all that he has done!'